Lake Oswego Jr. High
2500 SW Country Club Rd.
Lake Oswego, OR 97034
503-534-2335

Civil War
Battles

THE
CIVIL WAR
A NATION DIVIDED

THE CIVIL WAR
A NATION DIVIDED

Civil War Battles

Tim McNeese

CHELSEA HOUSE
PUBLISHERS
An imprint of Infobase Publishing

CIVIL WAR BATTLES

Copyright © 2009 by Infobase Publishing

Chelsea House
An imprint of Infobase Publishing
132 West 31st Street
New York, NY 10001

Library of Congress Cataloging-in-Publication Data
McNeese, Tim.
 Civil War battles / by Tim McNeese.
    p. cm. — (The Civil War: a nation divided)
 Includes bibliographical references and index.
 ISBN 978-1-60413-034-8 (acid-free paper)
 1. United States—History—Civil War, 1861–1865—Campaigns. I. Title.

 E470.M458 2009
 973.7'3—dc22   2008026561

You can find Chelsea House on the World Wide Web at
http://www.chelseahouse.com

Series design by Lina Farinella
Cover design by Takeshi Takahashi

Printed in the United States of America

Bang NMSG 10 9 8 7 6 5 4 3 2 1

This book is printed on acid-free paper.

Contents

Chronology

1820   The Missouri Compromise allows Maine to be admitted to the Union as a free state and Missouri as a slave state in 1821.

1831   William Lloyd Garrison publishes the first issue of his abolitionist newspaper, *The Liberator*.

1836   The House of Representatives passes a gag rule that automatically tables or postpones action on all petitions relating to slavery without hearing them.

1838   The Underground Railroad is formally organized.

1845   Former slave Frederick Douglass publishes his autobiography, *Narrative of the Life of Frederick Douglass, An American Slave*.

1850   Congress enacts several measures that together make up the Compromise of 1850.

1852   Harriet Beecher Stowe publishes *Uncle Tom's Cabin*.

1854   Congress passes the Kansas-Nebraska Act, which overturns the Missouri Compromise and thus opens northern territories to slavery.

1855   As Kansas prepares to vote, thousands of Border Ruffians from Missouri enter the territory in an attempt to influence the elections. This begins the period known as Bleeding Kansas.

1856   South Carolina representative Preston Brooks attacks Massachusetts senator Charles Sumner on the Senate floor and beats him with a cane.

1857 The Supreme Court rules, in *Dred Scott v. Sandford,* that blacks are not U.S. citizens and slaveholders have the right to take slaves into free areas of the country.

1859 John Brown seizes the arsenal at Harpers Ferry, Virginia. Robert E. Lee, then a Federal Army regular, leads the troops that capture Brown.

1860 **NOVEMBER** Abraham Lincoln is elected president.

DECEMBER A South Carolina convention passes an ordinance of secession, and the state secedes from the Union.

1861 **JANUARY** Florida, Alabama, Georgia, and Louisiana secede from the Union.

FEBRUARY Texas votes to secede from the Union. The Confederate States of America is formed and elects Jefferson Davis as its president.

MARCH Abraham Lincoln is sworn in as the sixteenth president of the United States and delivers his first inaugural address.

APRIL 12 At 4:30 A.M., Confederate forces fire on South Carolina's Fort Sumter. The Civil War begins. Virginia secedes from the Union five days later.

MAY Arkansas and North Carolina secede from the Union.

JUNE Tennessee secedes from the Union.

JULY 21 The Union suffers a defeat in northern Virginia, at the First Battle of Bull Run (Manassas).

AUGUST The Confederates win the Battle of Wilson's Creek, in Missouri.

1862 **FEBRUARY 6** In Tennessee, Union general Ulysses S. Grant captures Fort Henry. Ten days later, he captures Fort Donelson.

MARCH The Confederate ironclad ship CSS *Virginia* (formerly the USS *Merrimack*) battles the Union ironclad *Monitor* to a draw. The Union's Peninsular Campaign begins in Virginia.

APRIL 6–7 Ulysses S. Grant defeats Confederate forces in the Battle of Shiloh (Pittsburg Landing), in Tennessee.

APRIL 24 David Farragut moves his fleet of Union Navy vessels up the Mississippi River to take New Orleans.

MAY 31 The Battle of Seven Pines (Fair Oaks) takes place in Virginia.

JUNE 1 Robert E. Lee assumes command of the Army of Northern Virginia.

JUNE 25–JULY 1 The Seven Days Battles are fought in Virginia.

AUGUST 29–30 The Union is defeated at the Second Battle of Bull Run.

SEPTEMBER 17 The bloodiest day in U.S. military history: Confederate forces under Robert E. Lee are stopped at Antietam, Maryland, by Union forces under George B. McClellan.

SEPTEMBER 22 The first Emancipation Proclamation to free slaves in the rebellious states is issued by President Lincoln.

DECEMBER 13 The Union's Army of the Potomac, under Ambrose Burnside, suffers a costly defeat at Fredericksburg, Virginia.

1863

JANUARY 1 President Lincoln issues the final Emancipation Proclamation.

JANUARY 29 Ulysses S. Grant is placed in command of the Army of the West, with orders to capture Vicksburg, Mississippi.

MAY 1–4 Union forces under Joseph Hooker are defeated decisively by Robert E. Lee's much smaller forces at the Battle of Chancellorsville, in Virginia.

MAY 10 The South suffers a huge blow as General Thomas "Stonewall" Jackson dies from wounds he received during the battle of Chancellorsville.

JUNE 3 Robert E. Lee launches his second invasion of the North; he heads into Pennsylvania with 75,000 Confederate troops.

JULY 1–3 The tide of war turns against the South as the Confederates are defeated at the Battle of Gettysburg in Pennsylvania.

JULY 4 Vicksburg, the last Confederate stronghold on the Mississippi River, surrenders to Ulysses S. Grant after a six-week siege.

JULY 13–16 Antidraft riots rip through New York City.

JULY 18 The black 54th Massachusetts Infantry Regiment under Colonel Robert Gould Shaw assaults a fortified Confederate position at Fort Wagner, South Carolina.

SEPTEMBER 19–20 A decisive Confederate victory takes place at Chickamauga, Tennessee.

NOVEMBER 19 President Lincoln delivers the Gettysburg Address.

NOVEMBER 23–25 Ulysses S. Grant's Union forces win an important victory at the Battle of Chattanooga, in Tennessee.

1864

MARCH 9 President Lincoln names Ulysses S. Grant general-in-chief of all the armies of the United States.

MAY 4 Ulysses S. Grant opens a massive coordinated campaign against Robert E. Lee's Confederate armies in Virginia.

MAY 5–6 The Battle of the Wilderness is fought in Virginia.

MAY 8–12 The Battle of Spotsylvania is fought in Virginia.

JUNE 1–3 The Battle of Cold Harbor is fought in Virginia.

JUNE 15 Union forces miss an opportunity to capture Petersburg, Virginia; this results in a nine-month Union siege of the city.

SEPTEMBER 2 Atlanta, Georgia, is captured by Union forces led by William Tecumseh Sherman.

OCTOBER 19 Union general Philip H. Sheridan wins a decisive victory over Confederate general Jubal Early in the Shenandoah Valley of Virginia.

NOVEMBER 8 Abraham Lincoln is reelected president, defeating Democratic challenger George B. McClellan.

NOVEMBER 15 General William T. Sherman begins his March to the Sea from Atlanta.

DECEMBER 15–16 Confederate general John Bell Hood is defeated at Nashville, Tennessee, by Union forces under George H. Thomas.

DECEMBER 21 General Sherman reaches Savannah, Georgia; he leaves behind a path of destruction 300 miles long and 60 miles wide from Atlanta to the sea.

1865 Southern states begin to pass Black Codes.

JANUARY 31 The U.S. Congress approves the Thirteenth Amendment to the United States Constitution.

FEBRUARY 3 A peace conference takes place as President Lincoln meets with Confederate Vice President Alexander Stephens at Hampton Roads, Virginia; the meeting ends in failure, and the war continues.

MARCH 4 Lincoln delivers his second inaugural address ("With Malice Toward None"). Congress establishes the Freedmen's Bureau.

MARCH 25   Robert E. Lee's Army of Northern Virginia begins its last offensive with an attack on the center of Ulysses S. Grant's forces at Petersburg, Virginia. Four hours later, Lee's attack is broken.

APRIL 2   Grant's forces begin a general advance and break through Lee's lines at Petersburg. Lee evacuates Petersburg. Richmond, Virginia, the Confederate capital, is evacuated.

APRIL 9   Robert E. Lee surrenders his Confederate Army to Ulysses S. Grant at the village of Appomattox Court House, Virginia.

APRIL 14   John Wilkes Booth shoots President Lincoln at Ford's Theatre in Washington, D.C.

APRIL 15   President Abraham Lincoln dies. Vice President Andrew Johnson assumes the presidency.

APRIL 18   Confederate general Joseph E. Johnston surrenders to Union general William T. Sherman in North Carolina.

APRIL 26   John Wilkes Booth is shot and killed in a tobacco barn in Virginia.

DECEMBER   The Thirteenth Amendment is ratified.

1866   Congress approves the Fourteenth Amendment to the Constitution.

Congress passes the Civil Rights Act.

The responsibilities and powers of the Freedmen's Bureau are expanded by Congress. The legislation is vetoed by President Johnson, but Congress overrides his veto.

The Ku Klux Klan is established in Tennessee.

1867   Congress passes the Military Reconstruction Act.

Congress passes the Tenure of Office Act.

1868   The impeachment trial of President Andrew Johnson ends in acquittal.

Ulysses S. Grant is elected president.

1869   Congress approves the Fifteenth Amendment to the Constitution.

1871   The Ku Klux Klan Act is passed by Congress.

1872   President Grant is reelected.

1875   A new Civil Rights Act is passed.

1877   Rutherford B. Hayes assumes the presidency.

The Reconstruction Era ends.

Bull Run (Manassas)

For four straight years, the people of the United States fought one another in a brutal war. The Civil War would result in the deaths of about 620,000 men in uniform. More Americans died during this bloody nineteenth-century conflict than in all other American wars combined. They fought on battlefields across the South and on Northern soil in Maryland, Pennsylvania, Missouri, and Kentucky (even though that state's government was officially neutral).

The war's battles are nearly countless, ranging from minor skirmishes to full-scale engagements that sometimes stretched across battlefields measuring miles in length. Some of those battles would become key to the overall outcome of the war and revealed the honor of the armies that clashed across bloodied ground. Sometimes these battles displayed the limits of a man's endurance and the frayed ends of his ability to cause death, watching it up close and personal. The story of these battles is the story of the men who risked their lives for a personal cause. In the end, some of those men paid the ultimate sacrifice.

The U.S. Civil War had been decades in coming. For most of the first half of the nineteenth century, the United States was expanding into a continental nation, one spanning from the Atlantic to the Pacific. During this time, a great debate was swirling over the issue of the expansion of slavery. By mid-century, one out of every seven people living in the United States was a black person held in permanent bondage.

In the North, where limited slavery had existed during the colonial era of the 1600s and 1700s, many people did not feel that slavery had an impact on their lives. Many Northerners were not opposed to Southerners holding slaves. They simply did not want to see the "peculiar institution" spread into the territories as more and more Americans migrated into the vast open lands of the West. The expansion of slavery had divided the country and had been the focus of constant debate and congressional argument. Congressmen had written up repeated compromises that allowed slavery in one place while denying it elsewhere.

POSTPONING A CERTAIN OUTCOME

The arguments over slavery's expansion merely put off what was sure to happen. By the 1850s, the issue had turned white hot. A new political party, the Republican Party, had been established in 1854. They were nearly all Northerners who opposed the expansion of slavery into the western lands. When they nearly elected a president in 1856 without a single Southern vote, Southerners panicked. Then, Republicans elected Abraham Lincoln from Illinois. Many Southerners believed he was not only opposed to slavery's expansion, but to even the existence of slavery. Because of this, when he was elected, they chose to leave the United States altogether.

In December 1860, South Carolina seceded from the Union. Over the following six months, another 10 Southern states joined with it to form their own country, the Confederate States of America. When the newly inaugurated President Lincoln insisted that the U.S. government have control over federal lands in the South, Southerners in Charleston, South Carolina, decided to fire on a federal fort out in the city's harbor—Fort Sumter. On the morning of April 12, 1861, Confederate artillery batteries opened fire and bombarded the Union stone fortress for 36 straight hours until it surrendered. The Civil War had begun.

Meanwhile, both sides had already gathered massive armies for the coming fight. Many thought a single large battle might actually determine the outcome of the war. To hurry that battle along, a Union army that was gathered outside Washington, D.C., was sent across the Potomac River toward the Rebel capital of Richmond, Virginia. The battle that unfolded would become the first major field engagement of the war.

PLANNING THEIR STRATEGIES

When the two armies met on the ground that would become the battlefield of Bull Run, both commanders came with the same strategy in mind: to attack one another's right side. The leader of the Union forces was Brigadier General Irwin McDowell; the leader of the Confederates was Brigadier General Pierre G.T. Beauregard, who had commanded Southern forces during the bombardment of Fort Sumter. Since they both had the same idea for an attack, it was important who went first.

McDowell made the first offensive steps on the morning of July 21, which caused Beauregard to abandon his plans. The Union commander's attack plan called for an operation that would swing several miles to the northwest before dawn and then cross a local stream known as Bull Run at Sudley's Ford. The Union men were to then turn toward the southeast and attack Beauregard's flank. McDowell anticipated that the Confederates would retreat in the face of the Yankee advance, as more Union troops crossed the creek and joined in the overall assault against the Rebels. All did not go according to plan.

The first significant battle of the Civil War occurred when Union and Confederate forces met at Bull Run in Virginia. Although both sides were disorganized and undisciplined, Union general Irwin McDowell pushed to seize an advantage over Southern forces. Despite his efforts, the Union Army was not successful in its first charge against the Confederacy (above).

Prior to the attack, General McDowell was uncertain of its timing. The Union Army was still a largely unorganized force that faced constant supply shortages and a lack of transport wagons. That summer, commanders were still identifying regiments (organized groups of a large number of soldiers), and dividing them into the smaller units called brigades. By the time McDowell's army moved southward on July 16, beginning the Union's "Forward to Richmond" campaign, many of his men were coming close to the end of their original 90-day service contract, called an enlistment. In fact, in the days just before the approaching battle, an infantry regiment and artillery battery finished their enlistments and left to go home. On the Confederate side, soldiers had signed up for longer enlistment periods, so there was little possibility of losing men before a fight. This perhaps gave the Southerners a psychological advantage going into the battle.

Even as McDowell marched out of Washington, D.C., Beauregard knew he was coming. Here, in the early months of the war, a significant spy network was already well established in the nation's capital. It provided information, as historian James McPherson describes, through "coded messages carried by southern belles riding fast steeds." Despite knowing what was coming, Beauregard would have to fight against the Union troops without expectation of help from General Joseph Johnston, who was in command of all Confederates troops in Virginia.

All the newly enlisted men on both sides were green and inexperienced in the arts of war. These early soldiers, carrying their 50-pound (23-kilogram) packs, were easily tired out and required three days to cover the same distance on foot as troops later in the war covered in just one. Thus, McDowell's advance out of Washington moved excruciatingly slow and faced constant delays. There was also a lack of discipline as soldiers, tired of waiting along a dusty Virginia road, wandered out of formation to search for wild animals to hunt or a water supply. By the time they reached Centreville, Virginia, McDowell's men had eaten all the food in their packs, causing the march to stop and wait while new rations were delivered by wagon.

The Union Army suffered from other shortages, as well, such as a lack of well-trained cavalry. Infantry troops are soldiers who travel and fight on foot, while cavalry are those who travel and fight on horseback. Many of the Union's best cavalry commanders and enlisted men were from the South and they had left Union service to defend the land of their births.

McDowell himself had to go out and scout the terrain to see where Beauregard's men were located. Once he found them, he realized they were strung out across rugged and difficult terrain and had built good defense systems in case of direct assault. This led McDowell to abandon his plan of attacking the Confederate right flank. Instead, he decided to attack their left. Because of all its delays, the Union Army did not attack before the morning of July 21, which gave the Rebels enough time to deliver by train an additional three brigades to the future battleground.

Nevertheless, when McDowell did attack, he and his green forces came close to a quick and clear victory. Beauregard, prior to the battle, had spread out his men along the south banks of Bull Run, which flowed just a matter of miles north of Manassas Junction, a rail town. On the Confederate right, troops held a railroad bridge, while their comrades on the left had control of another bridge, crossed by the Warrenton Turnpike. Six miles (10 kilometers) of rolling Virginia land separated Beauregard's two flanks. Prior to the fight, the Southern commander anticipated McDowell would attack along the railroad line, which led him to position 9 of his 10 and a half brigades along his right side. From there, he intended to launch his own attack before McDowell could make his first offensive move. But the Union commander beat him to it.

FIRST TO THE FIELD

McDowell had ordered his men up and ready for their first major battle at 2:00 A.M. His army numbered 10,000, a large force for early in the war, but one that would soon be dwarfed in later battles. He sent them forward through the local underbrush to attack the Confederate left. To draw the attention of the Confederates away from his main group, he ordered a few leftover regiments to make obvious moves toward the turnpike bridge. In the meantime, McDowell's larger army crossed Bull

Color Confusion on the Battlefield

When the Civil War opened in the spring of 1861, so many men volunteered for military service, the war departments of both armies were soon overwhelmed. They experienced shortages of everything needed for their new troops, from knapsacks to guns to socks. Lifting some of this strain on supply for both armies was the fact that a considerable number of the troops that would make up the early armies were militiamen from the various states. These men were already uniformed and supplied for fighting. However, each militia unit had its own type of uniform, including its own unique colors. When all these colors mixed on the early battlefields it sometimes caused confusion.

During the Battle of Bull Run, one of the largest of the early battles, a pair of Union cannon batteries was firing at the Confederate line when a regiment of blue-uniformed soldiers appeared just 70 yards (65 meters) away from the Union artillery units. When the Union artillerymen realized these were not their comrades, but rather Confederate soldiers, it was too late. The Confederates fired at the Union artillery, killing them and silencing their guns. From that point on, the Northern attack wavered and fell into confusion.

The flags carried by various units could also be a problem, due to their similarities. Historian James McPherson notes the problem: "With 11 stars on a blue field set in the corner of a flag with two red and one white horizontal bars, the Confederate 'stars and bars' could be mistaken for the stars and stripes in the smoke and haze of battle." It was because of these similarities that General Beauregard, who commanded Southern troops during the Battle of Bull Run, designed a different flag. Beauregard placed 11 stars for the 11 Confederate states on the blue "X" of St. Andrew's Cross, set against a red field background. This flag would become the famous Confederate flag during the remainder of the war.

Run Stream a couple of miles upriver from the bridge, unseen by the enemy—almost.

Commanding Southern boys assigned to the railroad bridge was a South Carolinian colonel, Nathan "Shanks" Evans. (He earned his nickname from his skinny legs.) Evans was a hard-edged soldier who felt that McDowell's fake move toward the bridge was not the one to watch. Instead, he noticed dust rising above the trees along the route of the column along his left. Rather than wait, he ordered his forces forward. They managed to meet the Yankees out in open fields and delay the Federal attack long enough for two additional Confederate brigades to reach the fight. All along the ground north of the turnpike, a two-hour fight raged between 4,500 Southern troops and 10,000 Union men. Despite how inexperienced the troops on both sides were, they stood their ground well and fought as if they had done so before.

One problem for both sides was the inexperience of their officers, who missed opportunities on the battlefield and sometimes poorly coordinated their portion of the battle. Coordination was a constant problem between the units fighting on the same side. Some of the officers who were engaged in the fighting would one day become famous. On the Union side, such leaders as Oliver O. Howard, Ambrose E. Burnside, and William Tecumseh Sherman were on hand. The Confederate officers included not only Beauregard and Joe Johnston, but also the most flamboyant cavalry leader of the South, James E.B. "Jeb" Stuart. Historian James McPherson describes Stuart as "the dashing, romantic, bearded, plumed, and deadly efficient colonel." Then, there was Thomas J. Jackson, the oddball math instructor from the Virginia Military Institute. Jackson came to Bull Run commanding a Virginian brigade from the Shenandoah Valley, where Jackson would fight Yankees over and over again for the next two years.

As the two armies fought hard, the larger number of Yankee men was having an impact on the battle. Outnumbered Rebels were pushed across the turnpike and back to the sloping ground of Henry House Hill. (The rise was named for a local invalid widow named Judith Henry, who before the battle had refused to leave her home. She was later killed when an artillery shell hit her house.) Some Southern units simply gave up and fled to the Confederate rear in a panic. On neighboring hilltops, Northern supporters had come out of Washington to witness the great battle, which many thought would determine the outcome of the war that very day. Spectators had come out in wagons, in surreys, and on horseback. They included members of Congress and their families, carrying picnic lunches to enjoy during the battle and make a day of their Sunday outing. They were 2 miles (3 km) from the battle, so from their lookout point they actually saw little but smoke rising from the distant field. Had they been closer, they might have seen that General McDowell was about to pull off a stunning victory against Beauregard's Confederate Army.

Expectations of a Rebel defeat at Bull Run would soon be disproved. During the fighting, generals Johnston and Beauregard had sent reinforcements to strengthen the Confederate left flank and had even taken up positions at the front to direct the battle up close and personal. The temperatures rose to sweltering heights that day while the battle raged, with both sides launching attacks and counterattacks across Henry House Hill.

STONEWALL

It was on Henry House Hill that the tide began to turn for the Confederate Army. The man responsible would be Thomas J. Jackson. The Virginia Military Institute professor was considered odd, obsessed with his own health and imagined illnesses, and he drove his men hard throughout the war. He was a Presbyterian with strong beliefs who brought no sense of humor to his command; he believed he was fighting God's own holy war against the North. He had not yet become the Confederate

Suffering from a lack of supplies, a large turnover of soldiers, and inexperienced leaders, neither side was completely prepared at the start of the Battle of Bull Run (above). Though Union forces under the command of General McDowell were initially successful in pushing back Confederate troops, the South soon gained the upper hand and defeated the Federal soldiers.

commander of legend, but he was about to make his name on the widow's hill. One by one, through the heat of the day, Rebel units had retreated across the battlefield away from the fight, away from the superior numbers of Yankees in their path. Jackson and his men arrived late on the field, around noon, and took up positions at the crest of Henry House Hill.

As they fought, they held the hill even as others fell back to safer positions, exhausted after hours of battle. But Jackson's men held their ground. Their stand was noticed by another Confederate officer, General Barnard Bee, from South Carolina, who

was losing the field as his men were starting to retreat. According to historian James McPherson, Bee shouted to his troops,
"There is Jackson standing like a stone wall! Rally behind the
Virginians!" General Jackson's men were holding their portion
of the Confederate line when most other units were giving up
the fight. Jackson, hereafter remembered as "Stonewall," and his
men became a rallying cry, and the Confederate Army began to
hold its positions. The time was mid-afternoon, and McDowell's
forces were struggling to hold on to their earlier gains, having
fallen into confusion and disorder. Blue-uniformed Northerners began to give up and retreat back to their rear lines.

Then, the Union commander failed to deliver two fresh
brigades to the field. The Confederates soon received reinforcements, the last of the remaining troops from the Shenandoah
Valley, who arrived by train that afternoon around 4:00 P.M.
This evened out the manpower each side had available on the
battlefield. (Before the battle was over, both North and South
had delivered 18,000 men to Bull Run). The Confederate Army
could not only match the North man for man on the ground,
but it had many more fresh troops than the Federals. According to historian James McPherson, as exhausted Union men
watched the Rebels gain fresh forces, some observed: "Where
are our reserves?"

Seeing the advantage for himself, perhaps for the first time
since the battle had opened, General Beauregard ordered a
counterattack against the disorganized and tired Yankees. With
the force of a rising tide, the Rebels began pushing the Northern
troops off the field and into a full-blown retreat. Panic overcame
the Federals. To lighten their loads and make their escape to
safety, many Union men abandoned all their equipment, including guns, packs, and everything else they no longer needed.

Still, just as Jackson had stood his ground earlier in the day,
not all the Northern troops fell into retreat. William T. Sherman's
brigade largely stood its ground and formed a rear guard that
helped hold back the advancing Rebels. The Southern fighters

began to shout out an odd scream that would become known as the Rebel Yell. It would become a sound Union armies would come to dread. Noted by historian Bruce Catton in his book *Glory Road*, one Union veteran tried to describe the eerie cry of the Southern soldier: "There is nothing like it on this side of the infernal region. The peculiar corkscrew sensation that it sends down your backbone under these circumstances can never be told. You have to feel it."

The defeat of the Union Army would later be referred to as the Great Skedaddle. Union soldiers, trying to make for the main road back to Washington, collided with the civilians who had come out to watch the fight. Historian Samuel S. Cox quotes Congressman Albert Riddle, who was on the scene:

> We called to them, tried to tell them there was no danger, called them to stop, implored them to stand. We called them cowards, denounced them in the most offensive terms, put out our heavy revolvers, and threatened to shoot them, but all in vain; a cruel, crazy, mad, hopeless panic possessed them, and communicated to everybody about in front and rear. The heat was awful, although now about six [in the evening]; the men were exhausted—their mouths gaped, their lips cracked and blackened with the powder of the cartridges they had bitten off in the battle, their eyes starting in frenzy; no mortal ever saw such a mass of ghastly wretches.

For the North, the day had turned against them. Yet, even though the Southern army had won, both sides emerged from that hot, hectic fight with one clear understanding: One battle would not decide the war, and the conflict was going to be long and bloody.

Shiloh

In the early months of 1862, the war in the western parts of the South took center stage. Both presidents Lincoln and Davis were intent on controlling Kentucky, which hinged on the control of three key rivers in the region: the Mississippi, Tennessee, and Cumberland. Davis sent experienced veteran General Albert Sidney Johnston to Kentucky, where he engaged in battles in January against Union commanders Henry Halleck and Don Carlos Buell.

A BORDER STATE ENGAGEMENT

The Confederates were defeated at Mill Springs, Kentucky, which helped Union forces hold onto eastern Kentucky. Western Kentucky was a different story. The Tennessee and Cumberland rivers flowed through the region and into Ohio. Two Rebel forts, Fort Henry on the Tennessee and Fort Donelson on the Cumberland, blocked Union access up those rivers. General Ulysses S. Grant changed this. Grant, who was under Halleck's command, managed to capture both Fort Henry and Fort Donelson by mid-February. Although General Johnston was not present at either fort, the commanders he had installed at both were.

Following the twin defeats at Fort Donelson and Fort Henry, Johnston pulled his forces out of their positions in Kentucky and sent them southward, across the width of Tennessee, to Corinth, Mississippi. This was territory where Union forces were not as plentiful or menacing. His 27,000 men were soon reinforced by order of President Davis with troops sent from New Orleans and Pensacola, Florida. This increased the size of his field forces to about 42,000. All this maneuvering took place with General Grant unable to lift a military finger. Considering Grant's success in the field, it was ironic that his superior, General Halleck, became jealous and was determined to take command of Grant's forces himself. Temporarily, he removed Grant from command. Halleck had already profited from Grant's successes, taking credit for them and receiving a promotion to commander of all Union forces west of the Appalachian Mountains.

Halleck's next step was well planned. He returned Grant to field command and sent him to Pittsburgh Landing on the Tennessee River, about 20 miles (30 km) outside Corinth, to catch up with Johnston. Grant obediently led his Army of the Tennessee to Pittsburg Landing, a march that took about a month. They arrived at Pittsburg Landing on April 3. Grant was to stay there until he was reinforced by General Don Carlos Buell's 35,000-man force. Once the two armies were massed as one, General Halleck intended to join them, take command, and lead the Federals against Johnston's army at Corinth. But Halleck, of course, had not discussed this with Confederate general Johnston, who had no intention of waiting until Grant and Buell massed their men into a single force. Johnston determined to attack Grant before Buell had an opportunity to reach his Union colleague.

THE APPROACH OF BATTLE

Thanks to reinforcements, Grant's forces were counted at 42,000 men before the battle opened on April 6. They were spread among six divisions, five of which were encamped at Pittsburg Landing and the sixth about 6 miles (10 km) away at Crump's Landing. Some of Grant's men were struggling with illnesses, including dysentery, brought by the wet spring weather. As Rebel scouts delivered more reports of Northern troop movements and the approach of Buell toward Grant, General Johnston decided he must move—and quickly. But heavy spring rains slowed his march out of Corinth, and the attack was postponed to the following day.

By the evening of April 5, several of the officers under Johnston's command, among them General P.G.T. Beauregard, pleaded with him to call off the attack. They were certain their approach had been detected due to its slow pace. Beauregard was particularly concerned that, as noted by historian James McPherson, "the noise made by rebel soldiers firing off their guns to see if rain-dampened powder still worked had eliminated all chance of surprise." (However, since Union men were firing off their guns for the same reason, it is unlikely Grant's men would have realized they were hearing Confederate firing.) If Union forces knew the Confederates were coming, they would be already settled in and ready for a fight. Some Confederate officers were also concerned that Buell had already arrived to reinforce Grant. (Although a few of Buell's men had reached Grant already, the vast majority of them had not.) But Johnston would not hear of it. He was determined to meet Grant at Pittsburgh Landing. Historian James McDonough recalls Johnston's words: "I would fight them if they were a million. . . . Gentlemen, we shall attack at daylight tomorrow."

Johnston's lack of concern worked out well for his side. The Federals, in fact, had no idea the Confederates were approaching. General William Tecumseh Sherman, Grant's senior officer, received information about Rebel troop movements, but he did

After General Ulysses S. Grant heroically led his troops through Kentucky, he was ordered to bring his men to Pittsburg Landing, Tennessee, to await reinforcements before embarking on another campaign. Confederate forces, however, planned a successful surprise attack and initiated the Battle of Shiloh (above) and the fight for control in Tennessee.

not believe they were headed toward the Federal encampment. Instead, he was certain the Rebels would remain in Corinth and wait until the Union forces came to them. When a Union colonel speculated to Sherman that the woods in front of him could be crawling with thousands of Confederates, the gruff Union commander turned angrily on him, as noted by historian John K. Duke: "Beauregard is not such a fool as to leave his base of operations and attack us in ours." Sherman was wrong, and so was Grant, who also did not suspect the approach of Johnston's forces. When the battle began, Grant's men were not in defensive positions at all. Rather, they were scattered around the Tennessee hills in little camps that they had established to be close to water and available firewood.

"WE WILL WATER OUR HORSES IN THE TENNESSEE"

Just before dawn on April 6, a clear, beautiful Sunday, Johnston sent three of his six corps of Confederate troops along a line facing the enemy, telling his staff officers, as noted by historian Geoffrey Ward: "Tonight we will water our horses in the Tennessee River." Before anyone could change the field arrangement, the fighting began. It appears that, although Sherman and Grant had ignored claims that Rebel forces were close, other Union commanders had not. One of those regimental commanders, General Benjamin M. Prentiss, an Illinoisan who had fought in the Mexican-American War, had nervously sent out a patrol to scout for Confederates. They quickly crashed into the Rebel line and the battle was on.

Thousands of Confederates rushed out of the wooded area around the Shiloh church on the morning of April 6. The landscape was difficult, rugged, uneven, and covered with woods. Five of Grant's divisions were scattered across the slopes along the river, and his sixth, under the command of General Lew Wallace, was away from what would become the field of battle, at

Crump's Landing. None of Grant's forces had dug into trenches and gotten ready, since the Union commander had thought only of offensive moves.

The Rebels slammed into two inexperienced divisions, those of Sherman and General Grant. Sherman's forces, encamped near a small Methodist log church called Shiloh, were taking their breakfast and hurriedly reached for their muskets. Historian Geoffrey Ward notes the response of a Union private named Stilwell as the attack opened: "As I rose from the comfortable log from behind which a bunch of us had been firing, I saw men in gray and brown clothes, running through the camp on our right, and I saw something else, too . . . a gaudy sort of thing with red bars . . . a Rebel flag."

As noted by McPherson, a surprised Sherman shouted: "My God, we're attacked!" Next to him, his orderly was shot and killed. But the Union general recovered quickly and remained collected through the next 12 hours of fighting. He moved on horseback along his lines, ordering his green troops to fill gaps and even counterattack. The daring Sherman had three horses shot out from under him that day and was slightly wounded twice. Prentiss's forces held their ground, too, until the other three divisions on the scene reinforced them.

As for Grant, he, too, had been sitting down for breakfast when the air was shattered by rifle and cannon barrages. He was also nowhere near the battle, but instead was 9 miles (15 km) downriver at his headquarters waiting for Buell's arrival. Immediately, he took a dispatch boat upriver to Pittsburg Landing, reaching the fight around 9:00 A.M. Before him, the whole country was at war on a scale that had not yet taken place between North and South.

A RETREAT FOR THE NORTH

Johnston's original plan of attack had been to hit the Union left side with a fury, push it back into the Union center, and then force Grant to retreat into a narrow pocket of swampy ground. But heavy Union resistance made that impossible. It was no help to Johnston, as well, when Confederates fell out of their ranks to ransack abandoned enemy encampments for food and other goods. Such actions by many Confederates caused a general disorganization within Southern ranks.

On both sides, thousands of young soldiers, taking in their first taste of combat, were terrorized by it. Between the two armies, four out of five soldiers had never seen a fight before, much less one of the scale that this battle would become. Many on both sides fled the field, leaving commanders to try and fill the gaps in their lines and reorganize their brigades. By the end of the day, 5,000 Union soldiers had retreated back to the Tennessee River and were huddled underneath a bluff.

Grant moved along his lines, taking counsel with all his divisional commanders throughout the day and ordering new lines of resistance and the movement of artillery units all along the ridgeline west of Pittsburg Landing. Johnston, too, put himself in the thick of the fight, moving down to the front lines along the Confederate right to bolster his men and drive them forward. An especially volatile portion of the line developed at a site later called the Hornet's Nest. It lay along the center of the battle lines, where Union men from Illinois and Iowa were situated, positioned along thickets by a sunken road. Twelve times, Confederates troops assaulted the Hornet's Nest, and each time they were pushed back.

Then, at mid-afternoon, Johnston was seriously wounded as he led a charge against Union positions in a peach orchard to the left of the sunken road. Here, as at the Hornet's Nest, the fighting was furious, even as soldiers were showered with pink flowering peach petals. Johnston took a bullet that severed his femoral artery, located behind the knee. The Rebel commander was taken off his horse, removed from the field, and died at about 2:30 that afternoon. He had simply bled to death. There

Caught unaware, Union soldiers camped at Pittsburg Landing were quickly orga-nized into a strong defensive line under the leadership of Union general Ulysses S. Grant. A well-known veteran of the Mexican-American War, Grant was actively involved in the battle and bravely ventured out to the front line to fight alongside his troops (above).

had been no doctor to see to his wound, since he had just sent one away to go and care for some enemy wounded.

The fighting, of course, went on, and the Confederates pushed forward. At the Hornet's Nest, the fighting remained hard and desperate. Prentiss's line of men was turned back on both flanks, leaving Confederates to attack from three sides. There were 62 Rebel cannons concentrated at that point on the battlefield, "the largest concentration of artillery yet assembled in an American war," notes historian Geoffrey Ward. General Prentiss was finally overwhelmed around 5:30, forcing his surrender, along with 2,200 or so of his men. The Union Army was retreating along its entire line. Grant rushed about, looking for General Wallace and reinforcements. They never came.

Late in the day, around sunset, some of General Buell's regiments reached the banks of the river opposite Pittsburg Landing and were ferried across by steamboat. Grant's forces had taken serious casualties through the day of intense fighting. His effective fighting force had been reduced to about 18,000 men, all formed together in a tight position around Pittsburg Landing. Grant's position was shaky, and he knew it. He had his back to the river, with little room to maneuver, and his forces were tired, battered, and down in number. The Federals positioned themselves for yet another Confederate assault. But it did not appear. General Beauregard, now in command, pulled his forces back, certain he would be able to annihilate his enemy the following morning. He allowed his men to ransack the abandoned Union encampments.

THE LONG NIGHT

Both armies struggled through a long night, one marked by heavy rains that began around midnight. Thousands of wounded Northerners and Southerners lay together across the miles of battlefield, since no system had yet been developed to organize the removal of the wounded under a flag of truce. Men cried in pain through the night. Lightning flashes revealed that wild hogs were feeding on the bodies of the dead. Some wounded men found water in a muddy hole close to the peach orchard. They died on its banks, their blood spilling into the water. It would be named Bloody Pond.

The Union men still able to fight were in a tight spot. With the river to their backs, they could not evacuate overnight, nor did Grant intend to do so. According to historian Bruce Catton, in his book *Grant Moves South*, when several of the officers under Grant's command suggested an evacuation across the river before a second day of fighting could take place, Grant was unmoved. He reportedly stated: "Retreat? No. I propose to attack at daylight and whip them." Grant chose to remain in the encampments near Pittsburg Landing, rather than take a cabin in one of the Union steamboats. He could not sleep due to the cries of the wounded men scattered for miles across the day's field of battle. Sherman found him later under a tree in the rain. Historian Geoffrey Ward recalls their simple exchange:

"Well, Grant," Sherman said. "We've had the devil's own day, haven't we?"

"Yes," Grant answered. "Yes. Lick 'em tomorrow."

The Union commander was as confident as he could be concerning the following day, when the battle would resume. Grant ordered an all-night barrage from his gunboats on the Tennessee River against Confederate positions. Throughout the evening, large numbers of Buell's men reached Grant's positions, having finally arrived down the Tennessee River. The men stepped onto the river's banks to a regimental band playing "Dixie." General Wallace's men, who had wasted the day by being lost, also arrived. In all, Grant was reinforced with 27,000 men, including 20,000 of Buell's and Wallace's 7,000. But the key to the next day would not be their number; rather, it was that they were fresh troops, those who were not weary from the previous day's hard fight. Grant intended to launch his own attack on the morning of April 7.

Over in the Confederate encampment, Beauregard was just as confident as Grant about the day of fighting to come. He occupied General Sherman's tent near the Shiloh church, where he would sleep soundly that night. That evening, he sent a telegram to President Davis in Richmond informing him of a great victory in Tennessee, as noted by historian James McPherson: "After a severe battle of ten hours, thanks be to the Almighty, [we] gained a complete victory, driving the enemy from every position." For Beauregard, the following day would simply serve as a clear conclusion of a fight that had only ended early because night came. Of course, Beauregard was unaware of the reinforcements Grant had already received.

One Confederate leader who was not as confident as Beauregard about the next day was cavalry commander Nathan Bedford Forrest. His men scouted Union positions that evening and into the night, watching as steamboats delivered thousands of Buell's men to Pittsburg Landing. When Forrest set out to inform Beauregard of this new piece on the chessboard of battle, he could not find him. Other Southern generals he did meet with did not take his information that seriously.

Nathan Bedford Forrest: The Last Man Out

The battle at Shiloh was a massive encounter that resulted in more American casualties in two days than had taken place in all other previous American wars combined. Because of the severity of the conflict, General Grant did not want to send Union forces to follow the retreating Confederates. However, he did send General William Tecumseh Sherman down the road of Rebel retreat toward Corinth to give chase to the Confederate forces. Although that march would accomplish little, it did help create a legend involving a Southern cavalry commander that would continue to grow through the course of the war.

Nathan Bedford Forrest was a Southerner of humble origins, who made a fortune in cotton and in buying and selling land and slaves. When the war broke out, he immediately set out to enlist volunteers for a cavalry unit he would command. He outfitted his entire battalion out of his own pocket.

APRIL 7

Grant ordered his men forward at 7:00 A.M., and they faced little resistance for their first mile of ground gained. The Confederates had abandoned that territory to plunder the Union camps. Once the Union men reached the full force of Confederates, the fighting resumed to an intensity that soon matched and would even exceed the previous day. But the advantage was in Union hands. Buell's fresh forces moved along the Union left flank and drove the tired Confederates back across the peach orchard. The Rebels then turned and counterattacked, and the fighting soon seesawed over the same ground until the Federals finally broke Confederate resistance and drove them into retreat.

As Beauregard's men retreated from the Shiloh battlefield, it was Forrest's cavalry that provided protection. The Rebel evacuation was slowed due to muddy roads. With Sherman's men closing in, General Forrest turned and ordered a cavalry charge. What happened next became the stuff of Forrest legend, as noted by historian Ward:

> Forrest ordered one last charge, swinging his saber and galloping headlong into the Union troops, only to discover that his men were not following him. Caught in a swarm of blue uniforms, Forrest whirled, slashing at the Yankees who tried to stop him, and was hit in the back by a musket ball. Despite the shock and pain, he managed to lean down and haul a trooper across his saddle to serve as a shield as he galloped away. Once out of range, he hurled his terrified protector aside and rode on toward Corinth.

Sherman did not pursue the Confederates any longer and soon returned to the former battlefield, having accomplished almost nothing. As for General Forrest, he recovered from his wound and lived to serve the Confederacy throughout the remainder of the war. He continued to live by his personal motto, remembered by historian Ward: "War means fighting. And fighting means killing."

When additional Union soldiers poured into the area to reinforce their fellow troops at Pittsburg Landing, the Confederate Army began to break apart and lose its ground. Finally ordered to retreat, Rebel forces abandoned the shelters and camps they had seized in the initial surprise attack that started the Battle of Shiloh. Union men returned to these shelters and were able to rest and recover after the fighting had ended (above).

Meanwhile, the Rebels were overwhelmed on the Union right flank, where Grant himself led his own army and Wallace's men stood in the forefront. The Confederates lost one field position after another south of Owl Creek. One of their units, led by Major General Braxton Bragg, held its ground stubbornly where the Corinth and Hamburg-Purdy roads crossed along the battlefield's center. Here, the action became white hot as Grant and Buell both ordered repeated attacks along Water Oaks Pond. The musket fire was withering. Historian Steven Woodworth notes that the fighting "became so intense that Sherman said it was the heaviest he had ever heard." For five hours, from 7:00 A.M. until around noon, the furious battle raged until Beauregard ordered a general retreat.

As the Federals advanced over ground that had seen battle the previous day, they encountered a terrible sight in the wounded and dead who had spent the night in the field unattended. Bodies were everywhere. Some of the wounded had found one another throughout the long night and huddled in groups for warmth. One Northern soldier would write later, as noted by historian McDonough: "Many had died there, and others were in the last agonies as we passed. . . . Their groans and cries were heart-rending. . . . The gory corpses lying all about us, in every imaginable attitude, and slain by an inconceivable variety of wounds, were shocking to behold."

By 2:00 P.M. or so, nearly the entire Union line had pushed the Confederates back to the place where the previous day's attack had begun. At 2:30, Beauregard's chief of staff offered a question to his commander, recalled by historian Thomas Jordan: "Do you not think our troops are very much in the condition of a lump of sugar thoroughly soaked with water, but yet preserving its original shape, though ready to dissolve? Would it not be judicious to get away with what we have?" Beauregard could only accept the analogy and agree, issuing a final retreat order. Even as the Confederates moved off the field and down the road back toward Corinth, the Union men were not ordered to pursue them. In his memoirs, General Grant addressed the reasons:

> After the rain of the night before and the frequent and heavy rains for some days previous, the roads were almost impassable. The enemy, carrying his artillery and supply trains over them in his retreat, made them still worse for troops following. I wanted to pursue, but had not the heart to order the men who had fought desperately for two days, lying in the mud and rain whenever not fighting, and I did

not feel disposed positively to order Buell, or any part of
his command, to pursue.

As the enemy disappeared down a muddy road toward
Corinth, relieved and victorious Union forces simply collapsed,
exhausted from the fight, many of them back in the encampments they had surrendered the previous morning. The battle
was over.

Just days after this great fight in the woods of western Tennessee, Halleck finally arrived and immediately took command
from Grant, the victor of Shiloh. Halleck did not pursue the
enemy immediately but waited until Major General John Pope's
army came with reinforcements. He then took the combined
forces of Grant, Buell, and Pope—a mass of 100,000 men—on a
slow campaign toward Corinth. His march took six weeks, since
Halleck insisted that his army build elaborate trenches every
quarter mile (400 m) or so, to avoid being exposed to an enemy
attack. By the time Halleck reached Corinth, Beauregard and
his forces were long gone. For many, the now legendary Shiloh
campaign ended unsatisfactorily. Union men felt they had lost
an opportunity to destroy Beauregard's army, while the Confederates, including President Davis, were sorry the Rebel commander had given up the vital rail center of Corinth without a
fight.

What had begun as a seemingly sure Confederate win over
Grant's army had ended after a second day as a major Rebel
defeat. The first anniversary of the start of the Civil War was just
days away, and Shiloh was the largest battle to take place thus far.
It was the first engagement of a size that would become commonplace during the next three years of the national conflict.
About 20,000 men were killed or wounded at Shiloh, with each
side taking about the same number of casualties. This was, as
noted by historian James McPherson, "nearly double the 12,000
battle casualties at Manassas, Wilson's Creek, Fort Donelson,
and Pea Ridge *combined*."

Both sides realized that the war in the western theater would be long and even bloodier before it was over. Historian James McPherson notes one Union soldier's prediction prior to Shiloh: "My opinion is that this war will be closed in less than six months." That same Federal observed after Shiloh: "If my life is spared I will continue in my country's service until this rebellion is put down, should it be ten years." Even Grant had thought before Shiloh, as he noted in his *Memoirs*, that one large-scale Union victory following his capture of Fort Donelson and Fort Henry might bring the war in the West to an end. After Shiloh, he "gave up all idea of saving the Union except by complete conquest."

The Seven Days

The Battle of Shiloh helped strengthen Union positions and an overall Union presence in western Tennessee. Grant would remain in the region and pursue new goals against the Confederates, targeting the Mississippi for Union control. This would lead to his campaign against the last major Confederate stronghold on the great river's course: Vicksburg. These campaigns would preoccupy Grant until the summer of 1863.

"ON TO RICHMOND"

Back in the eastern theater of the war, General George McClellan was preparing to mount his "On to Richmond" campaign, which he had been planning the previous winter. His strategy called for Union troops to move along the Virginia peninsula, east of the Confederate capital, from Fort Monroe. The eastern flowing rivers would provide cover for their flanks toward Richmond. His army was immense, amounting to 120,000 men supported by 15,000 horses and mules, 44 artillery batteries, 1,100 wagons, and a vast array of military equipment and hardware. The plan was a brilliant one. Unfortunately, George McClellan was the one who would carry it out.

By late March, McClellan's forces were in place at Fort Monroe to take up the westward march toward Richmond. His advance units reached Yorktown on April 5, the day before General Albert Sidney Johnston began his attack against Grant at Shiloh. McClellan believed he was outnumbered and slowed his forces immediately. In reality, Union forces outnumbered Confederate defenders at Yorktown four to one. McClellan's forces remained almost motionless for an entire month.

Finally, in May, McClellan moved, reaching the outskirts of Richmond by the end of the month. On May 31, the Federals engaged a Confederate force under the command of General Joseph Johnston. This became a two-day battle called Fair Oaks, or Seven Pines. Although Rebel forces did well early on, they were finally overwhelmed by superior numbers of Union men. But the key result of the Fair Oaks battle was the severe wounding of General Johnston, who had to be replaced by a veteran of the U.S. Army, General Robert E. Lee. At that time, Lee had not led masses of men into battle during the Civil War. He would soon prove himself as the greatest general of the war.

General Lee's reputation as a field commander during the Civil War began during the Seven Days fighting. He took command on June 1. Immediately, he set out to checkmate the threat McClellan's army represented to Richmond. Since Lee was significantly outnumbered by the Union forces in front of him, any offensive Confederate plan would have to be daring and bold.

Lee placed a thin line of troops to man the defensive lines between the Union Army and Richmond. At the same time, he intended to concentrate the bulk of his army against only one Union corps, the 5th, commanded by Major General Fitz John Porter. It was Porter's proximity to the Chickahominy River

With his top military officer injured and unable to lead, Confederate president Jefferson Davis turned to generals Robert E. Lee (left) and Stonewall Jackson (right) to lead the rebels against Union general George McClellan and his troops. Lee, who knew the Confederate Army was outnumbered, organized an offensive strategy against McClellan that required both generals to attack with their units at two different locations.

that attracted Lee's attentions. With the Chickahominy separating Porter's forces from the main body of McClellan's army, it would be difficult for McClellan to reinforce the 5th in time.

McClellan had sent Porter north of the river to provide protection for the Union Army's supply line, which followed the Richmond & York River Railroad, leading to a rail depot at White House Landing, along the Pamunkey River. McClellan did not feel he had placed Porter in a difficult spot by leaving him isolated on the other side of the river: The 5th had taken up a good defensive position along a swampy creek bottom. But Lee knew better than McClellan just how vulnerable Porter's forces really were.

LEE'S PLAN OF ACTION

Lee's plan would involve Stonewall Jackson, who was off to the north distracting three separate Union armies so they could not turn south and reinforce McClellan. Lee secretly ordered Jackson to swing south and strike against Porter on his flank, while Lee would throw his army directly against Porter's front. It was a gamble, indeed. His plan concentrated 60,000 Confederates against Porter's 30,000. With the bulk of McClellan's army south of the Chickahominy, it would also provide an opening for the Union commander to order his remaining 75,000 men forward toward Richmond with only 27,000 Rebel troops in front of them. If McClellan took that simple step, Richmond might fall and all might be lost. But Lee knew McClellan and judged him to be a commander who would not take the risk.

Lee went on the offensive on June 26, the second day of the week of fighting that would come to be called the Seven Days. The previous day, McClellan had thrown some of his men, the 3rd Corps, under the command of Major General Samuel Heintzelman, against Lee's men who held the ground directly in front of Richmond. It was McClellan's attempt at judging the strength of Lee's defensive line. The Confederate 3rd gave strong resistance, causing more than 500 casualties among the Union men while only taking about 300. McClellan judged the resistance at his front to be significant, and he wired Washington to demand more troops. He had no idea that Lee had actually concentrated his men toward the Union right.

McClellan, however, was not totally in the dark. He had received word that Jackson had turned south and was headed toward his army. Still, he had no real idea of the true strength of Lee's forces or even their accurate number. On June 25, the day he ordered the probe to test rebel strength at his front, he also sent a telegram to Edwin Stanton, the Union secretary of war, as noted by historian James McPherson in his book *Battle Cry of Freedom*: "The rebel force is stated at 200,000, including Jackson

Fighting a Black Man's War

Early in the war, President Lincoln refused to allow black men to enlist in the military. He was concerned that allowing blacks to fight would hurt relations with slavery supporters in the four border states. However, as the war took its toll and the number of casualties climbed on the Union side, some Union generals began organizing free Northern blacks and fugitive slaves into African-American units. Such black military units were meant at first to provide labor, rather than combat roles. Once Lincoln issued his Emancipation Proclamation in the fall of 1862, he finally accepted the idea of black enrollment in the U.S. military.

As black men were accepted into the Union Army, they faced discrimination. At first, segregated troops were commanded by white officers. In time, black soldiers demanded officers of color, and eventually nearly 100 black officers were stationed among the [it was actually less than 90,000] . . . I shall have to contend against vastly superior odds. . . . If [the army] is destroyed by overwhelming numbers . . . the responsibility cannot be thrown on my shoulders; it must rest where it belongs."

But even as Lee planned to attack on June 26, the battle did not begin according to plan. Jackson was to strike against Porter's army early in the morning, but he did not arrive on the field in time. The pressure on Lee was significant. He had just taken command from the wounded Joe Johnston and needed to prove himself. Also, Confederate president Jefferson Davis had ridden out of the capital to watch Lee's offensive in action. Jackson proved to be a no-show, and his attack did not open that morning or any other time that day. The reason for his failure to reach the field remains somewhat a mystery even today.

166 black regiments. None, however, was given a rank higher than captain. Also, at first, black soldiers were not given pay equal to what white soldiers received. Food allotments to black units also were less than to whites, and medical care was not as good. As a result, black soldiers suffered twice the death rate from disease as white soldiers.

Black soldiers were also treated differently by the Confederacy. Rebel officials threatened to execute or force into slavery any captured black soldiers. When Lincoln vowed to order the execution of a white Confederate prisoner for every black soldier killed, Southern leaders officially changed their policy. There were exceptions, of course, such as when black soldiers were massacred by Confederates following the April 1864 Battle of Fort Pillow in Tennessee.

From 1862 until the end of the war, nearly 180,000 black men served in the U.S. Army, while another 10,000 served as sailors. Overall, 82 percent of the eligible black men in the North enlisted in the U.S. military. The roles carried out by black soldiers and the sheer numbers of those who served demonstrates that blacks provided an important contribution to the Union war effort.

Another of Lee's generals, Ambrose Powell "A.P" Hill, felt his patience with Jackson reaching a breaking point. Not to lose the day completely, Hill chose to launch his own offensive that day. Hill's position on Lee's left flank put him closest to Porter's forces. But Hill's characteristic impatience cost him and his commander. As Hill's men moved forward, the remainder of Lee's army thought Jackson had arrived and they, too, stepped forward against the Union enemy, only to be pushed back. A Confederate force of 14,000 soldiers had tangled with about 15,000 or 16,000 Union men in the Battle of Mechanicsville. The Rebels lost more than 10 percent of their men on the field that day. Union losses added up to only a quarter of how many the Confederates had lost. The day had proven to be a frustrating tactical failure for Lee.

TO GAINES' MILL

Even though McClellan's forces won the engagement that day, he never considered going on the offensive against the Confederates himself. Jackson was near Porter's army, and so McClellan wisely ordered Porter to move his men 4 miles (6.5 km) back to a better position on higher ground along Boatswain's Swamp, outside another local community called Gaines' Mill. The troop movement took place through the night of June 26 to 27.

This move was significant. By moving Porter, McClellan figured that he had lost his supply line along the railroad line north of the Chickahominy River. This forced him to move his supply base along the James River on the southern side of the peninsula. The decision changed McClellan's basic strategy. He would have to give up plans to surround and bombard Richmond into surrender. This was the case, since his heavy weaponry could only be moved on rail flatcars and there was no railway near his new position along the James River. This meant the Battle of Mechanicsville might not have been a defeat for

Lee's forces, after all. The battle had forced McClellan to abandon the heart of his old attack plan.

Although Lee had made gains on June 26 at Gaines' Mill, he still needed to force Porter out of his positions behind Boatswain's Swamp. This meant that Lee's strategy on June 27 was generally the same as June 26. And, again, Jackson failed Lee. The attack on McClellan's right did not happen quickly enough. Once again, A.P. Hill's men pushed forward, attacking Porter's center positions, while taking serious casualties as they fought to cross through thick woods and a ravine that cut deeply across their path. Once again, the Federals were ready and waiting. It was a hot summer afternoon, and the only relief Hill received was from General James Longstreet's men and a few of Jackson's forces. It was not until close to sundown that Lee finally had all his men in position to move in a coordinated way toward the enemy.

When they did, the Federals found themselves facing a strong force. Lee concentrated greater numbers of troops against Porter's 5th Corps. Near the center of Lee's line were forces under the command of John Bell Hood, described by James McPherson in *Battle Cry of Freedom* as "a tall, tawny-bearded, gladiatorial brigadier." Hood's forces managed to break the Union line. Soon, with minutes of daylight ticking away, Porter's forces broke. The 5th was only saved by the fall of night and a few Union brigades that rushed in to protect Porter's retreat.

Lee had won, but the victory came with a high price. Union losses amounted to 4,000 killed or wounded, plus 2,800 captured. Lee's casualties were counted at 8,700. In six hours of afternoon and evening fighting, Lee had lost almost as many men as the Rebels had lost in two days of fighting at Shiloh.

ALONG THE CHICKAHOMINY

During those two days, June 26 to 27, the vast majority of McClellan's men had not seen much fighting. McClellan had sent 6,000 of them across the river to support Porter, but the remaining 69,000 Federal forces had remained nearly motionless. In part, it seems, they were nearly frozen with anticipation of what Rebel commander John Magruder would do.

A thin line of 27,000 of Magruder's men was the only force standing in McClellan's way of marching into Richmond. Magruder had managed to keep the Federals off balance by firing artillery and then moving cannons around to make it appear that the Rebels had more firepower than they actually did. Magruder did the same with his troops, moving them in and out of wooded areas to create the illusion of more men. He even had his officers with the loudest voices hide in the woods and shout out commands to troops that did not exist. McClellan and the officers under his command were completely bamboozled. All the action against Porter would not have mattered if McClellan had not misjudged the strength of the enemy directly in front of him. On the evening of June 27, McClellan had even wired Secretary of War Edwin Stanton to inform him that he had been "attacked by greatly superior numbers" from both sides of the Chickahominy River, reports historian James McPherson.

Although the Seven Days battles were not over yet, General McClellan was already thinking like a defeated commander. He had more men, had taken fewer casualties in two days than Lee, and could have pushed Magruder out of the way at any moment. The failure was McClellan's, but he blamed everyone and everything else. Four hours after his telegram to Stanton, the Union commander sent an angry, frustrated follow-up, recalled by James McPherson: "I have lost this battle because my force was too small. . . . The Government has not sustained this army. . . . If I save this army now, I tell you plainly that I owe no thanks to you or to any other persons in Washington. You have done your best to sacrifice this army." Fortunately for McClellan, perhaps, his full message never reached Stanton. A colonel in the telegraph office in Washington removed the last two lines from the general's telegram before handing the wire to Secretary Stanton.

Robert E. Lee exploited the weaknesses of his Union opponent, General George McClellan, a cautious leader who was reluctant to take risks in war. Although Lee managed to eliminate the threat of Federal occupation of Richmond, the Southern war hero lost an estimated 8,700 soldiers, more than double the number of Union soldiers. Above, injured Union soldiers from the Battle of Gaines' Mill sit on a flatbed railcar awaiting transport to the nearest hospital.

June 28 was spent moving around forces on both sides. On June 29, with all his men south of the Chickahominy, Lee attacked. He hit McClellan's rear guard, commanded by Major General Edwin Vose Sumner's 2nd Corps. Sumner's forces were at Savage's Station, 3 miles (5 km) south of the river, along the Richmond & York River Railroad, due east of Richmond. A ragged fight broke out, and Lee suffered from poor maps, bad geography, strong Union resistance, and failures by Magruder, who did not attack with full strength. In addition, once again, Stonewall Jackson spent much of the day having his troops rebuild a bridge rather than send his men to the battle. The result was a Confederate assault that was disorganized and half-hearted. Sumner was able to hold his ground. In part, his men fought to protect a Union hospital near Savage's Station where several thousand Federal troops lay wounded and sick. And yet, McClellan ordered Sumner to abandon his positions, leaving the hospital's 2,500 occupants as prisoners of war.

FROM GLENDALE TO SAVAGE'S STATION

Lee did not lose a day this time, choosing to bear down on McClellan. His rather complicated plan called for coordinated assaults by seven Rebel divisions outside the crossroads hamlet of Glendale, several miles southeast of Savage's Station. Lee believed that, if he could take Glendale and control the crossroads, he could split McClellan's forces just as the Chickahominy had. Then he could defeat the larger of the two halves. But, once again, coordination failed as only two divisions—one headed by Longstreet and the other by Daniel Harvey "D.H." Hill—were pushed into the battle against five Union divisions.

Incredibly, Jackson again failed to enter the fight as fully as expected. At one point during the battle, Jackson actually took a nap! Jackson's failure to really engage the enemy that day was "complete, disastrous, and unredeemable," notes historian Clifford Dowdey in his book *The Seven Days*. Again, the battle did not get going until late in the day.

But the fighting on June 30 would prove key to the Seven Days. The battle would be remembered by various names—Glendale, White Oak Swamp, Frayser's Farm, as well as several others. Federal troops fought hard for the crossroads and managed to hold out long enough to keep their positions. They did so even as McClellan, once more, shockingly ordered another retreat to the south toward Harrison's Landing on the banks of the James River. Lee finished the day frustrated. He had pushed the Union forces farther south, away from Richmond, but had lost another opportunity to crush McClellan's army. After days of heavy fighting, Lee now found himself facing an enemy that had moved repeatedly out of good defenses only to take up some of its best field positions yet.

UP MALVERN HILL

Malvern Hill stands 3 miles (5 km) south of Glendale, not far from the northern banks of the James River. It was an ideal position on which to make a stand, and the Federals knew it. The hill rose 150 feet (45 meters) in height and lay between two long ravines sitting a mile (1.5 km) apart. The only option for a commander who desperately wanted to fight the Union Army was to approach the hill in a direct frontal assault. This would place Lee's forces out in the open with McClellan's men occupying the high ground. From those heights, Union cannons could concentrate their deadly fire on the enemy. In all, four Union divisions backed with 100 artillery pieces were in position before the battle began, with an additional 150 guns waiting to take their places.

Lee had a decision to make. He could send his men up Malvern Hill or wait the enemy out. Lee would not wait. He and Jackson met early that morning to decide where to position Rebel cannons to maximize their firepower. But it was all for nothing. As noted by historian Steven Woodworth, "Union guns were larger, more numerous, better served, better sited, and supplied with better ammunition." Federal cannons destroyed Confederate artillery units before they even had an opportunity to get set up.

One factor that led Lee to launch the attack was his sense that Union forces were already feeling whipped, and so, perhaps, was their commander, McClellan. There was evidence of this, Lee thought. As Federals had retreated from north of the Chickahominy toward Harrison's Landing on the James, they had abandoned a significant amount of equipment along the roads. Confederates had picked up 30,000 muskets and rifles,

The last of the fighting during the Seven Days battles occurred at a crossroads near Frayser's Farm in Virginia (above). Robert E. Lee, whose military orders were bungled by his unit commanders, hoped to completely destroy McClellan's army, but he was disappointed when the Union retreated farther into the South. The failures of the Union Army during the Seven Days battles were a shock to Northerners who had previously expected the Civil War to be a short-lived affair.

as well as 50 cannons. During six days of fighting, 6,000 Union men had been captured, including some that very morning. If McClellan's forces were as low on spirit as McClellan himself, Lee thought victory might still be within his grasp at Malvern Hill.

Once Lee ordered the infantry assault up the gently sloping hill, Federal forces were more than ready. The Rebel commander had ordered cannons of his own set up on two small hills north of Malvern's location, but staff problems caused some artillery units to get the message while others did not. For those who did take up their positions, they were soon blasted apart.

Lee would have to rely solely on the work of his infantry, men he sent marching up Malvern into the face of withering Federal firepower. Union artillery blasted apart Confederate units before they were even in good range for the rifles of the infantry. Lee lost 5,500 men, double the number lost on the Union side.

Incredibly, even as Lee had clearly lost the day, McClellan once again ordered another retreat. As noted by historian Bruce Catton, McClellan's reluctance prompted an officer under his command, Philip Kearny, to state angrily: "Such an order can only be prompted by cowardice or treason. . . . We ought instead of retreating to follow up the enemy and take Richmond."

The week of battles was over. Lee gave up his attacks, certain there was no way to defeat the Federals, especially given his losses: 20,000 men killed or wounded, a number equal to a quarter of his army, and twice as many as the Federals had lost. In some ways, the end of the week could not be explained. Union forces had only actually experienced one tactical defeat—the fight at Gaines' Mill—but they ended the week having retreated south of the Chickahominy. They abandoned their original rail supply line only to take up positions at Harrison's Landing, which put them in place for a full-blown abandonment of the peninsula. Richmond was safe, and Lee had saved it.

Despite his "success" during the Seven Days, Lee was not happy. His men had failed him, especially some of his commanders. Orders had not been delivered properly, and units had moved into position in a lazy fashion, and sometimes not at all. Commanders seemed slow to follow through on Lee's plans. He owed his success as much to McClellan's lack of nerve as to anything. According to historian Clifford Dowdey, Lee would write of the week: "Our success has not been as great or as complete as I could have desired. Under ordinary circumstances the Federal Army should have been destroyed."

The week of fighting resulted in nearly 35,000 casualties, including the wounded and those killed. This was a horrifying number at that point in the war, equal to the casualties farther west during the first six months of 1862, including the bloody Battle of Shiloh. Northern casualties amounted to 15,800 men compared to Lee's 20,100. The Seven Days would set the course for later battles that placed the North's Army of the Potomac against Lee's Army of Northern Virginia. These were engagements that required hard fighting and high casualties. In fact, throughout the war, "40 of the 50 highest-casualty regiments served in the Army of Northern Virginia," according to historian James McPherson. Lee would lead the pack as the commander with the highest casualty rate.

In the aftermath of the Seven Days, the direction of the conflict in the East would shift. Forced to give up his march to Richmond, one he had spent most of a year planning, McClellan was relieved of his command of the Army of the Potomac. He was replaced by General John Pope, who was certain he would quickly defeat Robert E. Lee, even before summer was over.

Antietam (Sharpsburg)

John Pope did not defeat Robert E. Lee during the Summer of 1862. Instead, he was roundly defeated by Lee and Stonewall Jackson in late August in a battle that unfolded on some of the same ground at Bull Run. With Lee's strategic victory at Second Manassas (Second Bull Run), the successful Confederate commander from Virginia set upon a new strategy. It was one that would take him outside of his native state. He was determined to take the war onto Northern territory. Once President Davis gave Lee's plan his blessing, Lee led his men on a march northward, crossing the Potomac River into Maryland at Leesburg, Virginia, on September 4, 1862. The Rebel general had hoped that the people of Maryland, a border state that allowed slavery, would celebrate his army as liberators. They did not.

A REPLACEMENT FOR POPE

In the meantime, President Lincoln had removed the failed General John Pope from command and shipped him out to Minnesota to fight Native Americans. Pope never led another army against the South. On September 2, Lincoln placed Mc-Clellan back in command of the Army of the Potomac. Learning that Lee had entered Union territory, McClellan took up his army and began marching toward the enemy on September 7, keeping his forces between Lee and Washington, D.C.

As Lee entered Maryland, he sent Stonewall Jackson and his forces to Harpers Ferry in western Virginia (today, this territory is the state of West Virginia). The Union had 10,000 soldiers stationed there with the ability to threaten Lee's supply lines. To send Jackson's army to Harpers Ferry, Lee had to divide his army. This would put him in a weaker position in the case of a Union attack. The Confederate general hoped the troops at the Union military post at Harpers Ferry might retreat, or that McClellan might be slow in pursuing the Southern forces. Neither proved true. In fact, on September 13, two Union soldiers discovered a piece of paper wrapped around three cigars at an abandoned Confederate camp outside Frederick, Maryland. It was a lucky find for McClellan: The paper was a copy of Lee's Special Orders No. 191, which revealed that Lee had split his army. Armed with this information, McClellan knew he must get to Lee and attack before Jackson had an opportunity to reunite with Lee.

Although McClellan did move his forces faster toward Lee, he did not move quickly enough. A friendly Marylander informed Lee of McClellan's newly discovered information, and the Confederate general quickly sent messengers to instruct Jackson to rejoin Lee's forces as soon as possible. By September 15, the Union post at Harpers Ferry surrendered, and Jackson set out to catch up with Lee. The following day, with the Federals approaching, Lee drew up his men outside Sharpsburg, Maryland, along the west bank of Antietam Creek, and prepared to fight. It was a questionable choice of location that Lee had made. He had the Potomac River to his back, which would cut off any necessary retreat, just as Grant had fought at Shiloh with the Tennessee River to his rear. Lee hoped that McClellan would command his men badly, as he had during the Seven Days, the

September 17, 1862, marked the start of the Battle of Antietam (above) *and the bloodiest day of the Civil War. General Robert E. Lee had hoped to win the battle to further his army's advance into Northern territory, but the Union gained a critical advantage when they discovered Lee had divided his army to cover more ground. When the fighting was over, Lee had lost approximately one-quarter of his army to death and injury.*

only previous time McClellan and Lee had fought one another as commanders.

On September 16, McClellan's advance guard reached Lee's lines, but the Union commander only poked at Lee's army, failing to attack with full force. McClellan's timid actions would not serve him well. By the following day, all of Lee's men, minus one division, had reached the fields west of Antietam and were ready to fight. Before their arrival, Lee had only three divisions manning his line. On the morning of September 16, McClellan had 60,000 men available for an attack against Lee and 15,000 more within 6 miles (10 km) of Antietam Creek. By comparison, Lee had only 25,000 or 30,000 men in position. Had McClellan attacked in full a day or two earlier, he might have crushed Lee's army completely. But he had not.

At 5:30 in the morning on September 17, Union general Joseph Hooker, organized on McClellan's right, did move forward. The Battle of Antietam had begun.

STRATEGIES AND GENERALS

Southerners would give the fight at Antietam the name "Sharpsburg." The battle was unique, according to historian James McPherson, because it "was one of the few battles of the war in which both commanders deliberately chose the field and planned their tactics beforehand." Neither side had time to dig into trenches, as Confederates took positions in tree groves, behind rocks and stone walls, and along a sunken road located at the Rebels' center. Along Lee's right stood a stone bridge that crossed Antietam Creek, which the Confederates fought desperately that day to hold.

McClellan sent three corps of men to the Union right, where the battle opened, and he sent General Ambrose Burnside toward the bridge on the Federal left flank. McClellan meant to catch Lee's attention so he would not station many troops on his left, where McClellan was concentrating his own men. In the meantime, the Union commander held back four additional divisions and much of his cavalry, planning to throw them into the fight if an opening exposed itself on his right flank or the center of his line. He also anticipated that Burnside would lead his men across the bridge and creek and crush Lee's right. The plan was a good one, but the battle did not unfold exactly according to plan.

Much of the blame for the plan's failure falls on McClellan and Burnside. McClellan did not coordinate his attacks well enough, which meant the battle unfolded in three stages, beginning on the Union right, then center, and finally on his left. This provided Lee the opportunity to shift his men during the battle in reaction to the series of three assaults that should have taken place more in unison than they did. In addition, Burnside wasted much of the day of the battle concentrating on capturing the bridge. He focused on this all morning and for much of the afternoon, even though his men could have simply waded across the creek against little Confederate opposition. Again, Lee was able to move a division that morning from his right to his left when the battle was most intense at that location, and then move them again back to his right when most of the fighting shifted in that direction. Lee simply outgeneraled McClellan that day. But the day would not end entirely in Lee's favor.

THE CORNFIELD

On the early morning of September 17, Hooker and his Union forces stepped forward, marching quickly down the Hagerstown Pike from the north, and soon engaged the enemy. Hooker was a veteran of the Mexican-American War, a hard-fighting general who liked to take the offensive and whose ego was legendary. He had gained his nickname, "Fighting Joe," from the Seven Days fighting. Hooker longed to command the Army of the Potomac some day, a desire he would live to see fulfilled.

Fighting on McClellan's right, Hooker's men pushed against the Rebel left, which was under the command of the newly arrived Stonewall Jackson. Much of the fight took place in the East Woods and across ground remembered later as "the Cornfield." Just north of the field was a whitewashed church of the German Dunkard sect, whose members were, ironically, pacifists. The corn was ripe and ready for harvest on that fall day, yet the rows of corn were cut to shreds by the intense level of musket fire from both sides.

At one point, Hooker's men appeared ready to roll back Jackson's men, but then the Rebels were reinforced. Lee sent

General D.H. Hill's division from the battlefield line's center and troops under General Longstreet's command from the Rebel right. It was the South's turn to push as Hooker's line fell back. Then, the Union 12th Corps carried out another assault, which broke the Confederates' line near the Dunkard church. This was followed closely by another Rebel challenge, which, once again, returned the Cornfield to Confederate control. It was again the Union's turn to take the field, which they did when General Edwin Vose "Bull" Sumner's 2nd Corps struck against the Rebels in the West Woods. The Rebels then returned the favor, countering with yet another charge through the woods and corn. This time the charge had more troops whom Lee had removed from his right, including some of Jackson's men who had only reached the battlefield that morning from Harpers Ferry.

The battle raged back and forth for five hours through the East Woods, the West Woods, and the Cornfield. In all, this part of the battle included five divisions on each side. Eventually, both sides, bloodied and badly damaged, broke off the fighting as cleanly as if their commanders had first sat down and made the decision together. The Confederate left had held. As for Hooker, he was removed from the battlefield, wounded. The musket fire through the field had been so intense that almost none of the cornstalks were left standing.

THE SUNKEN ROAD

Then, the battle shifted to the center of the line for both sides. General Sumner had made the first clear move in that direction, directing two of his divisions there before Confederates could approach his men from the left. The midday sun was high over the battlefield, and the battle's second phase began.

At this point on the battlefield, the action was centered along a portion of a sunken road. The Rebels had occupied this road before the battle, allowing them to use the low ground as a shallow-based trench of sorts and providing them with some real cover. The fighting went on for hours, with many casualties on both sides. Eventually, Northern forces managed to get the Confederates out of their positions on the sunken road. By then, the road was littered with the bodies of dead Rebel troops, which gave the battle site the name "Bloody Lane." With this break in the Confederate line, the Union men appeared to have an opportunity to destroy Lee's position.

The Virginia general scrambled for reinforcements, drawing them from other parts of the battlefield. Lee's decision was desperate, since moving men around left other parts of the fighting ground weakened. Fortunately for the Confederates, the reinforcements he shifted to his center saved his army from being destroyed. The fighting along the sunken road was just as ferocious as across the Cornfield. A Northern newspaper reporter was on the scene immediately after Union men pushed the Confederates back to the outskirts of Sharpsburg. He was stunned by what he saw, later writing, as noted by historian James McPherson, that the "Confederates had gone down as the grass falls before the scythe."

If McClellan had then sent some of his saved units toward the remains of the Confederate center, they would have found a clear path and extremely weakened Rebels. McPherson quotes one Rebel officer as writing later that "there was no body of Confederate infantry in this part of the field that could have resisted a serious advance." Another Confederate agreed, his words remembered by historian Frederick Tilbert: "Lee's army was ruined and the end of the Confederacy was in sight."

Given his opportunity, it is incredible that McClellan did not order another assault on the Confederate center. On the other hand, the commander of the Union's 6th Corps, General William B. Franklin, was eager to enter the fight. But with three Union corps exhausted after the fighting that morning, McClellan could not bring himself to order one more attack. He was also certain that Lee still had masses of troops saved up for a grand counterattack. McClellan ordered Franklin to stand down, saying, "it would not be prudent to make the attack," McPherson notes.

BURNSIDE'S BRIDGE

Late in the day, McClellan was still sending regiments, battalions, and even whole divisions bit by bit into the Antietam fight. Then the third phase of the battle opened along the Union left flank near the stone bridge. If McClellan was guilty that day of poor coordination and general bad management in this battle, he was not alone.

The commander of the Union's 9th Corps was Major General Ambrose Burnside. He was given orders to take his men across the Lower Bridge, otherwise known as the Rohrbach Bridge (today it is remembered as Burnside's Bridge). Perhaps the corps commander took his orders too literally. He wasted hours of combat time trying to capture the bridge from its defenders, while a brigade of Georgia boys, hiding in trees and behind a stone wall, pelted Burnside's line with bullets through the entire morning of the fight. General Robert A. Toombs was the commander of those Rebels, and the actions his men took at Antietam near the bridge would be his greatest achievement of the war. (Toombs had longed to be selected as the Confederacy's president, but he lost out to Jefferson Davis. It was a failure he never accepted, and he spent much of the war criticizing Davis.)

By mid-afternoon, a breakthrough came for Burnside. A pair of his best regiments finally made a desperate charge on the bridge and, despite many casualties, succeeded in their goal. Ironically, about that same time, other Union men found some sites to cross the river without the use of the bridge and made it to the other side that way. Soon, three divisions were steadily driving the enemy away from the river, back toward Sharpsburg. The Federals

The Confederacy's failure to occupy Northern territory in the Battle of Antietam boosted Union morale and allowed President Lincoln to issue the Emancipation Proclamation, a document that led to the end of slavery. Antietam became an important turning point in the war. Lincoln visited McClellan in his tent at Antietam (above) after the fighting had ended.

even threatened to cut off the road leading to the only spot the Rebels had for crossing back over the Potomac River to Virginia. The battle had finally turned completely in the North's favor.

Then, in a repeat of his cautious style of decision making on the field, McClellan considered sending in an entire reserve corps, the 5th, to relieve Burnside's men. According to historian Thomas M. Anderson, just as McClellan was about to send them in, their commander, General Fitz John Porter, warned his superior: "Remember, General, I command the last reserve of the last army of the Republic." (Porter later denied these words, although historians question his testimony.) With that, McClellan did not send the 5th Corps into the fight.

All along Lee's lines, his men were being driven back. It looked like defeat would be the result of the day of nonstop fighting. Then, he noticed in the distance a mass of men moving in his direction, masked by a whirl of dust. As noted by historian James F. Murfin, Lee was anxious to identify these new arrivals to the field. "Whose troops are those?" asked Lee. One of his officers pointed a telescope at them and finally answered Lee's question: "They are flying the Virginia and Confederate flags, sir." Lee could not have been more relieved. He had suffered throughout the day in the face of superior Union numbers, which allowed the Federals to send in fresh reinforcements repeatedly. Now, he was to have his own reinforcements.

The troops in question were General A.P. Hill's men, the last of those from Harpers Ferry. Hill had remained to work out a surrender with the Union commander and then rushed his men along the road to Sharpsburg. They reached the field of battle, taking on Burnside's men on the Confederate right side late in the day, just as those positions were falling into retreat. Surprised Federals soon turned in retreat. In part, the Union men did not fire on the approaching Confederates since many of Hill's men were wearing blue uniforms they had captured at Harpers Ferry. It is not an exaggeration to give Hill's men the credit for having saved the Army of Northern Virginia.

The day had become a bloodbath. All across the Sharps-burg battlefield, the bodies of 6,000 fighting men from both sides lay scattered in the Cornfield, along the sunken road, and near Rohrbach Bridge. In addition, 17,000 soldiers lay wounded. This number of casualties made Antietam the bloodiest single day of fighting of the entire war. Historian James McPherson notes that "more than twice as many Americans lost their lives in one day at Sharpsburg as fell in combat in the War of 1812, the Mexican War and the Spanish-American war *combined*." Several of Lee's brigades lost as many as 50 percent of their men to casualties, leaving only 30,000 Confederates able to fight in a possible second day at Antietam. Lee made no effort to remove them from harm's way. In part, this was because crossing the Po-tomac with that number of men was impossible. The following day, however, McClellan made no attempt to renew the battle. By evening, Lee ordered the return of his men back across the Potomac. Over the next several days, the Army of Northern Vir-ginia limped back to Southern soil.

General McClellan wasted no time declaring the battle a complete victory for himself. He sent Lincoln a message, claiming, as noted by historian James McPherson, "Maryland is entirely freed from the presence of the enemy, who has been driven across the Potomac. No fears need now be entertained for the safety of Pennsylvania." In a letter to his wife, McClellan shouted his own praises: "Those in whose judgment I rely tell me that I fought the battle splendidly & that it was a master-piece of art. . . . I feel that I have done all that can be asked in twice saving the country. . . . I feel some little pride in having, with a beaten & demoralized army, defeated Lee so utterly. . . . Well, one of these days history will I trust do me justice."

McClellan was right about one thing: The day was a victory for the Union, which had won the day under his command. Lee's army turned around and retreated from Union soil. In England, British officials had been closely watching the direction of the war and considering whether to enter the conflict by supporting the Confederacy. After the battle, British government officials decided to steer clear of such a commitment. President Lincoln, following the much-needed Union victory, took the opportunity to issue publicly his Emancipation Proclamation, which announced the freeing of slaves in Confederate-controlled territory. For these reasons, the battle would represent an important turning point in the war.

As Lee's men marched back to Virginia, it was his army that was feeling low. Nearly one out of every three Confederate soldiers who had marched into Maryland either did not return to Southern soil or had been wounded in battle. Lee's march into Maryland had proven a disaster. During the retreat across the Potomac, a Rebel regimental band began to play "Maryland, My Maryland." Not surprisingly, those who heard the tune raised a complaint, hissing and groaning. The band quickly selected a more appropriate tune: "Carry Me Back to Old Virginny."

Fredericksburg

Geneneral McClellan emerged peacock proud from his victory over Lee at Antietam. He had, indeed, taken the field that day and pushed Lee with his back to the Potomac. But he had not followed up his defeat of the major Confederate forces with a second day of fighting. In fact, he did not move his 100,000-man force for weeks following the battle, allowing Lee and the Army of Northern Virginia to escape completely across the river back into Virginia.

AN IMMOVABLE FORCE

During those weeks of inactivity, President Lincoln pleaded with his commander to take his army on the offensive. A typical letter from the president to McClellan was one dated October 6, which Lincoln sent to the general through General Halleck in Washington. Historian James McPherson quotes the communication: "Cross the Potomac and give battle. . . . Your army must move now while the roads are good."

Three weeks later, McClellan had not crossed the river. When Lincoln asked him to explain why, the general informed the president that his army's horses were tired and broken down. McPherson notes how Lincoln shot back a response: "Will you pardon me for asking what the horses of your army have done since the battle of Antietam that fatigues anything?" The overly proud Union commander ignored Lincoln, refusing to answer requests, demands, or orders. McClellan had won the battle but had failed to take his opportunity to possibly end the war.

Lincoln's patience would finally run out. In early November, the president took McClellan from his command of the

The Art of Deadly War

As Confederate and Union soldiers fought across battlefields from New Mexico to Maryland, the casualties mounted to dramatic numbers. Often, large-scale field encounters resulted in the deaths of hundreds, sometimes thousands of men, even if the fight lasted for only one day. Why was the casualty rate so high? The answer is not that complicated.

One factor that determined high casualty rates during the Civil War was the sheer number of men on the field. Nearly 39,000 soldiers were needed to defend 6 square miles (15 square kilometers) of ground. During World War I, that number had fallen to 4,000, and by the Persian Gulf War, it was fewer than a couple of dozen. Some Civil War battles involved more than 100,000 soldiers, or even twice that number, on a battlefield no bigger than a large university campus.

In addition, a wounded soldier had little possibility of recovering from his wounds. Civil War–era rifles and muskets had a low muzzle speed and used bullets of a large caliber (size). Bullets often

Army of the Potomac, replacing him with Major General Ambrose Burnside. The new commander was a West Point graduate and veteran of the Mexican-American War, and he had seen action most recently at Antietam and earlier at Second Bull Run. Perhaps, Lincoln hoped, Burnside would follow up the Antietam victory with another win against Lee and finish the job that McClellan had only started.

General Burnside was not McClellan, especially when it came to his ego. In fact, Burnside protested his appointment because he felt he was not ready for the role and its responsibilities. His modesty was a breath of fresh air to Lincoln. His new

remained in the victim's body rather than passing through in the way a modern copper-jacketed bullet does today. Getting the bullet out required the skills of a field surgeon working under primitive conditions, and there was a high risk of infection. There could be no operation on wounds to the chest, stomach, or intestines. Hits received in the arms or legs often shattered bones, making it impossible to set the limb. With the problem of infection and the severity of many wounds, amputation was commonplace. In 1866, the year following the end of the war, 20 percent of Mississippi's state income went to the purchase of artificial limbs for veterans.

In the hands of a skilled soldier, the weapons used to deliver such destructive wounds were often deadly accurate on the battlefield. The Civil War saw the wide use of rifles, which were considerably more accurate. Rifles typically fired a cone-shaped lead slug measuring a half inch (13 millimeters) in diameter and weighing 1 ounce. These were called Minie balls, after French army captain Claude Minie. The Minie ball tore through flesh and shattered bones when it struck its human target. Several of the rifles used could shoot only one bullet at a time before needing to be reloaded, but others held seven or more bullets. This provided the Civil War soldier with a destructive firepower that had never occurred before in wartime. The result was higher casualty rates.

general was, according to historian Steven Woodworth, "loyal, honest, brave, and competent within his limits. Unfortunately, commanding an army lay outside those limits."

Burnside moved his men immediately in the direction of General Lee's forces. He knew Lincoln would want him to pursue Lee before the onset of another winter froze both armies into position and paused the war until spring.

BURNSIDE IN COMMAND

On November 15, Burnside moved his massive army of 110,000 south toward Richmond, Virginia. They headed directly for Fredericksburg, which lies about halfway between Washington, D.C., and Richmond. Burnside hoped to reach the town along the banks of the Rappahannock River before Lee could reach it. He then planned to push farther southward and place his army between the Army of Northern Virginia and Lee's forces.

Within two days, Burnside had about one-third of his men at Falmouth, Virginia, on the north bank across the river from Fredericksburg. Lee's forces had not yet all arrived, so entering the town was only a matter of crossing the Rappahannock. However, the U.S. Department of War was slow in delivering pontoon boats to Burnside, which held him back from crossing the river. Burnside needed the pontoons to lay down a floating bridge across the river. In the meantime, Lee pushed his men to Fredericksburg, arriving at the town with 75,000 men between November 19 and 20. Burnside's pontoons had still not reached his field position. The delay waiting for boats had cost the Union Army dearly.

As Lee faced Burnside's army, he called for reinforcements from Stonewall Jackson, who was in the Shenandoah Valley with his corps. Jackson and his "foot cavalry" hit the roads at once for Fredericksburg. Meanwhile, Burnside called the town's mayor for a meeting and called on him to surrender Fredericksburg.

General Ambrose Burnside took control of the Army of the Potomac after Lincoln relieved General George McClellan of his command. Instead of continuing with McClellan's slow march into the South, Burnside took his forces on a campaign to attack and occupy Fredericksburg. Burnside directed Union engineers to place pontoon boats across the river to form temporary bridges (above).

The mayor refused, even in the face of Burnside's threat to blast the riverside buildings to pieces.

The Union commander provided 16 hours for the town to be evacuated before he began the bombing. When the mayor requested additional time, Burnside agreed. This delay gave

Jackson plenty of time to reach Lee, who had taken up field positions behind Fredericksburg at the top of a sloping hill called Marye's Heights. As for Burnside, his guns were established on the opposite banks of the river at Stafford Heights.

Little took place during the final week of November and even early December. Burnside was hesitant, talking with Lincoln regularly and putting off what was sure to happen. As Burnside settled on his strategy, he kept things overly simple. Lincoln suggested that he move his forces to use Fredericksburg as a turning point, not the direct target. But Burnside refused because he thought, as explained by historian James McPherson, that "the enemy will be more surprised by a crossing immediately in our front" across from Fredericksburg.

Burnside was wrong to plan things in such a simple way. For weeks, Lee and his lieutenants had hoped against hope that the Union commander would use so little imagination that he would order a direct frontal assault against the town and their forces dug into the ground behind it. Burnside chose to do just that. When the Federal attack finally opened, Lee had placed Longstreet's corps along a 4-mile (6 km) line of high ground overlooking the half mile (800 m) between the town and Marye's Heights. A stone wall 4 feet (1.2 m) high stood at the base of the hill, stretching for a half mile and providing cover for hundreds of Rebels.

During the weeks of delay and anticipation, both sides were dug into trenches in the ground so close to one another that some men could hear the conversations of their enemy. Sometimes Confederates and Union men even shared conversations. According to historian Geoffrey Ward, one Confederate officer recalled:

> We were attracted by one . . . of the enemy's bands playing . . . their national airs—the "Star Spangled Banner," "Hail Columbia," and others once so dear to us all. It seemed as if they expected some response from us; but

none was given until, finally, [they] struck up "Dixie," and then both sides cheered, with much laughter.

ACROSS THE RAPPAHANNOCK

On December 11, after weeks of preparation, what was perhaps the most anticipated battle of the Civil War took place. Burnside ordered his engineers to begin laying down pontoon bridges across the Rappahannock. Three bridges were to be built across from the town and an additional three a few miles downriver. The work downriver progressed well, with the engineers' efforts covered by artillery.

Those working directly across from Fredericksburg had a much more difficult time of things. Mississippi sharpshooters were in position in the storefronts and warehouses along the riverfront, picking off blue-clad engineers one by one. The Union engineers were driven from their work so many times that Burnside finally ordered the shelling of the town to drive the Rebel riflemen from their positions. But the Mississippi men did not immediately abandon their posts, and they continued to lay down harassing fire against the engineers. Frustrated, Burnside ordered troops to man the pontoon boats and row them across the river's width of 400 feet (120 m). Only then were the sharpshooters driven out of the town to rejoin the main Confederate force. Finally, the bridges in front of Fredericksburg could be placed without menace.

Throughout the remainder of the day and into a second, Union soldiers crossed the floating bridges into Fredericksburg. Civilians and Rebel soldiers alike had abandoned the town. The Union men, frustrated by the Rebel sharpshooters the previous day, rampaged through the houses, shops, and other buildings, taking everything they could. They destroyed everything they could not take, including furniture, glassware, and other domestic articles.

Two days after the bridge building had begun, the general was ready to march directly against Rebel lines at the top of Marye's Heights. Burnside's opponent held the high ground and had clearly seen the attack coming for some time. A direct frontal assault translated into suicide, but Burnside ordered one all the same. The field stretched for miles, and even before the Union attack, Lee had extended his lines by another 3 miles (5 km) by sending Jackson's corps up the Rappahannock to create an unbroken chain between Jackson's and Longstreet's men. So many Confederate gunmen and artillery units covered the ground up Marye's Heights that Longstreet quoted one of his cannon men as noting that "a chicken could not live on that field when we open on it."

"WE SHOULD GROW TOO FOND OF IT"

On December 13, the grand Army of the Potomac prepared to make its deadly march toward thousands of well-trained enemy guns. Burnside sent his forces toward Lee's army. At the far end of the Union line, General William B. Franklin's men faced Jackson. If Franklin could only manage to crush Jackson's right, other places along the Union line of attack—especially on its right flank along Marye's Heights—might be able to press through as well. But Franklin did not produce positive results that day. The efforts of his 50,000 men were weakened by Burnside's confusing orders and by Franklin's lack of drive to force the enemy out of position.

After the heavy ground fog lifted at mid-morning, Franklin's men hit Jackson's positions along Prospect Hill. On the Union left, Burnside had also sent Major General George G. Meade leading a division of Pennsylvania troops. Those troops discovered a break in Jackson's formations near a wooded ravine and, for a brief moment, took advantage of it and sent men into the break in the line. But Jackson's men rallied and soon drove the Union troops back outside their lines.

If Burnside had supported Meade, the Battle of Fredericksburg might have ended differently. In fact, Burnside did order Franklin to renew his assault against the enemy, but Franklin failed to respond to the order. He put only half of his men into the fight and was pushed back. Historian Douglas Southall Freeman recalls what General Lee said to Longstreet in response to the frenzied action on his right: "It is well that war is so terrible—we should grow too fond of it!"

Meanwhile, Burnside was also focusing on his own right side along Marye's Heights. Burnside had placed General Joe Hooker in charge of mounting the attack up the "Long Slope." It was here that the Union forces would meet furious fire from the Rebels, most of them positioned behind the stone wall and along a sunken road at the base of the heights.

The lay of the land made the direct frontal assault even more difficult than it would have been otherwise. A drainage ditch crossed the length of the heights. It was in a position such that the Union troops could only be sent up the slope one brigade at a time and then onto the portion of the field where Confederate firepower was most concentrated. Throughout the day, Burnside almost mindlessly sent troops charging up the hill with no hope of taking the field or pushing the Rebels off of it. One brigade after another was sent to its doom as the enemy poured shot at them, leaving bodies scattered across the ground, sometimes stacked two or three deep. As one newspaper reporter would write after the battle, according to historian Shelby Foote: "It can hardly be in human nature for men to show more valor or generals to manifest less judgment."

All told, Burnside ordered 14 assaults up Marye's Heights and all of them failed. Finally, near the day's end, the Union commander decided to call off the attack, finally certain the hill could not be taken.

By the time night fell across the bitter-cold battlefield, the ground west of Fredericksburg was littered with stacks of bodies. The day had delivered 13,000 casualties to the Union Army,

Burnside led the regiment into the Battle of Fredericksburg, a devastating event that resulted in approximately 13,000 Union casualties. Burnside's loss at Fredericksburg made his troops question his leadership in future campaigns like the Mud March (above).

about the same number it had suffered at Antietam. The difference was that Antietam had ended with a Union victory. On the Confederate side, the losses amounted to 5,300 men, the majority of them missing. Many of them had simply left the army after the fighting and headed home for Christmas.

The Battle of Fredericksburg ended with Ambrose Burnside weeping openly in front of his men, desperately pleading to lead one more charge with himself at the head of his old 9th Corps. It was not to be. The general had been beaten. Later, as he rode his horse past some of his men, one of his aides called for three cheers for Burnside. No one responded.

The night following the battle was one of misery and cold. The dead and dying were scattered across the immense field of battle. Men were removed from the field cautiously, since there was no agreement between the two sides on how to evacuate their comrades from the battleground. The night temperature fell to below freezing and a strong wind carried across the field. One of the wounded was Joshua Lawrence Chamberlain, the commander of the 20th Maine Volunteers and a former college professor. Historian Geoffrey Ward recalls Chamberlain's later written account: "It seemed best to bestow myself between two dead men among the many left there by earlier assaults, and to draw another crosswise for a pillow out of the trampled, blood-soaked sod, pulling the flap of his coat over my face to fend off the chilling winds, and still more chilling, the deep, many voiced moan that overspread the field." Chamberlain and many of his men lay on the field even the next day as Confederate snipers fired into the bodies there, trying to discover who might still be alive. That night sky of December 13 to 14 was lit up by the aurora borealis, the "northern lights," which are normally not visible that far south. Confederates viewed the eerie lights in the sky as a sign that God was blessing their efforts of the day.

When Burnside counseled with the officers under his command that night, he considered remounting the attack the following day. Fortunately, he was talked out of it. Instead, Robert E. Lee met with his officers, determined to launch a counterattack the next day against the Union forces he had bloodied already. A successful attack by the Rebels would have pinned Burnside against the Rappahannock, as Lee had been against the Potomac at Antietam. But the Northern army left its field positions and withdrew across the river through the night of December 14 to 15.

After the Union men evacuated Fredericksburg, Confederate troops came down from Marye's Heights to inspect the damage the Federals had done to the town. They found everything in chaos, destroyed, smashed, ransacked. Stonewall Jackson was among those who reentered Fredericksburg and was disgusted by what he saw. Historian Ward recalls Jackson's words when one of his officers asked him what men who do such things deserve: "Kill 'em. Kill 'em all."

Chancellorsville

Following the Battle of Fredericksburg, both armies slipped into winter quarters. For the Army of Northern Virginia, the year 1862 had delivered major battlefield victories, including the Seven Days, Second Bull Run, and Fredericksburg. Antietam had ended in defeat, but compared to the year the Federals had in the East—including the disaster that was Fredericksburg—Lee and his army had reason to hope that their cause might succeed.

For the Union men, spirits were extremely low. Then, when a January campaign failed due to heavy rains and mud, the Army of the Potomac sank even lower. There was a general agreement that General Ambrose Burnside was simply not up to the command he had been given. Some of his generals even campaigned for his removal. President Lincoln himself was also displeased with Burnside. Just two months after putting him in command, the president replaced Burnside with Major General "Fighting Joe" Hooker, who had seen action in several battles in the East.

HOOKER IN COMMAND

Hooker was not an easy choice for Lincoln. He had been one of the generals who sought Burnside's removal. As historian Steven Woodworth describes Hooker, he "combined extreme ambition with shocking political views and loathsome personal habits." He also, however, had a reputation as an aggressive war leader. Lincoln hoped he might therefore be the answer for the poor leadership under which the Army of the Potomac had suffered for more than a year and a half. But even as he selected Hooker for command, he wrote the general a letter, informing him that he had some misgivings about him. Woodworth notes the following from the letter:

> I have heard, in such way as to believe it, of your recently saying that both the Army and the Government needed a Dictator. Of course it was not for this, but in spite of it, that I have given you the command. Only those generals who gain successes, can set up dictators. What I now ask of you is military success, and I will risk the dictatorship.

Fortunately, Hooker took Lincoln's letter to heart and soon set out to rebuild the Army of the Potomac back to fighting strength, both physically and psychologically. Historian Geoffrey Ward recalls the words of one Union soldier: "Under Hooker, we began to *live*."

From winter to spring, Hooker showed himself to be a capable administrator and military organizer, plus he was a shot in the arm for his army's spirits. To encourage pride in his units, he began the practice of corps and division patches for their uniforms. He increased his army in size and outfitted them with the best equipment. According to Woodworth, the general often spoke of his forces as "the finest army on the planet." He also made it clear that he not only intended to engage the Confederate general Robert E. Lee come spring, he intended to defeat him. He often boasted, "May God have mercy on Bobby Lee, for I shall have none."

But all this retooling of his army and his personal boasting still needed to be backed up with a good strategy against the enemy and a victory in the field. As to his campaign strategy, he worked up a clear-cut plan of action against Lee. The plan called for one of his corps to distract Lee by crossing the Rappahannock near Fredericksburg, and then the remainder of the Union forces were to march to the west and turn to Lee's left flank. Then the Federals would make their own Rappahannock crossing, followed by a crossing of the Rapidan River before crossing into a thick woods referred to locally as the Wilderness. With their movements hidden by the dense underbrush, thickets, and vine-bearing trees, Hooker intended to emerge from the Wilderness and surprise Lee, with the Army of the Potomac between the Confederate general's forces and Richmond. Given Hooker's position, Lee would be forced to attack him at a location of the Union commander's choosing and would surely be defeated. Hooker was always absolutely sure of his plan, even as circumstances did not allow him to fully put it into operation when the time came.

OF WELL-LAID PLANS

By late April 1863, General Hooker was ready to put his plan and his army into action. On April 27, he sent Major General George W. Stoneman's cavalry out to harass Lee's lines and destroy rail lines at Lee's rear. Then he moved westward out of Falmouth, Virginia, to march around Lee with three corps: the 5th Corps under Major General George G. Meade; the 11th Corps, commanded by Major General Oliver O. Howard; and the 12th, General Henry Slocum's men. These three corps made up only a third of Hooker's army. By the following day, they reached the upper fords of the Rappahannock and crossed over at Kelly's Ford, which placed them 20 miles (30 km) upriver from Falmouth and at Lee's rear. Then, Hooker marched one of his corps to Germanna Ford and a second to Ely's Ford, both on the Rapidan River, a tributary of the Rappahannock. According to Hooker's plan, they then marched through the Wilderness to a major road junction at Chancellorsville. It was hardly a town, but a crossroads dominated by a large plantation home belonging to the local Chancellor family, plus a few other buildings and storefronts.

Meanwhile, Hooker left behind four corps at Falmouth. He ordered two of them, the 1st and the 6th, to cross the Rappahannock on April 29 with a great show. They were then to cross the river below Franklin's Crossing, where Burnside had sent his left flank over the river during the Fredericksburg campaign. Their purpose was to distract Lee while Hooker's other three corps on the move executed their turning movement against Lee's left flank. Then, Hooker's remaining two corps at Falmouth, the 2nd and 3rd, were to set out on a march to join up with the 5th, 11th, and 12th Corps, completing Hooker's elaborate maneuvering. The end result had Stoneman's cavalry at Lee's rear, three corps in place to turn to Lee's left, two additional corps hidden from Lee's view but prepared to cross once Hooker captured Chancellorsville, and his final two corps moving as obviously as possibe toward the Confederates.

For the most part, every portion of Hooker's strategy before the opening of the battle came together with no real problems. By April 30, Slocum and Howard were located south of the Rapidan at Germanna Ford and Ely's Ford. They then marched to the crossroads of Germanna Plank Road and the Orange Turnpike at Wilderness Tavern. That same afternoon, three corps were at Chancellorsville. The 1st and the 6th were in position along the Richmond Stage Road. Hooker could not have been more excited about his plans to whip Bobby Lee.

Chancellorsville was a key location in Hooker's plans. It was the home of a widow, Mrs. Sanford Chancellor, and her

General Joseph "Fighting Joe" Hooker's military experience made him an ideal candidate to lead one of the Union's best-known regiments, but his reputation was sullied by stories of his drinking and cavorting with women.

seven children, six of whom were unmarried daughters. Part of the family house was used as a tavern. The mansion was situated in the idle of a farm clearing, and it was virtually surrounded by thick woods. As recalled by historian Geoffrey Ward, one Iowa private described the Chancellor house as:

. . . of the Southern type, belonging to a well-known family of the neighborhood, still occupied by the women. Upon the upper porch was quite a bevy of ladies in light, dressy, attractive spring costumes. They scolded [us] audibly and reviled [us] bitterly. [Before] another day was over they would pitifully plead to be carried to a place of safety.

Hooker and his staff occupied the main floor of the house, certain they would complete their plan in another two days, bag Lee's army, and began their march to Richmond.

Even as Hooker's plan was unfolding during these final days of April, the key was whether Lee was falling for it all. Since the Battle of Fredericksburg months earlier, Lee had broken off three of his divisions from the main army and sent them to southern Virginia and North Carolina to fight. As to his remaining forces, Stonewall Jackson was encamped near Fredericksburg with four divisions, including A.P. Hill's Light Division, and three others commanded by General Raleigh Colston, a former French teacher at Virginia Military Institute; Jubal Anderson Early; and Robert Rodes. General James Longstreet was in command of two divisions, down from the five he had led at Fredericksburg. Hooker was aware of the three missing divisions and knew they would not have time to be summoned and return to Lee before the battle opened. This meant Lee had 60,000 soldiers available to him, about half the number Hooker was delivering across the region in and around Fredericksburg. As to the question of whether Lee was fooled by all the maneuvering of Hooker's forces, he was not.

A MARCH AROUND THE ENEMY

On May 1, Lee began to respond to Hooker's movements and was most concerned about the Union divisions at his left. He left General Early to keep watch over Fredericksburg and then marched the remainder of his army quickly to the west to hit Hooker before the Union commander could remove his men from the Wilderness. Lee was wise in choosing the woods for a fight because the thickness of the woods would make the great size of Hooker's force work against him.

The Union commander should have known this, and he should have known that he should move his men forward, out of the woods, onto open ground. However, even after skirmishing broke out between the two sides, Hooker not only failed to move his men out of the Wilderness, he actually sent them farther into the tangle of thickets and trees. Suddenly, Hooker's plan had changed. By remaining in the Wilderness, Hooker had given up the offensive and turned to a nonaggressive, defensive status. It was almost impossible to explain. According to historian Geoffrey Ward, Hooker would later explain himself, saying, "To tell the truth, I just lost confidence in Joe Hooker."

That evening, Lee and Jackson met to discuss a strategy for the following day's fight. Fortunately for them, General J.E.B. Stuart provided Lee with solid information from a cavalry spy mission. They then put together a plan that defined the boldness for which Lee was already legendary. Despite being outnumbered almost two to one, he decided to divide his army, sending 26,000 men under Jackson's command on a long, roundabout, 14-mile (23-km) route through the woods and along back roads to come in around the back side of Hooker's right flank. During the long-shot march, Lee was to keep Hooker busy and focused on his center. Jackson's march would take an entire day and Lee's reduced numbers would be in danger. Should Hooker organize himself for a full assault, Lee and his men might well be overwhelmed. The plan was desperate, gutsy, against the odds, and classic Robert E. Lee style.

On the morning of May 2, Jackson's forces headed southwest of Lee's center by a route that took them through the heavy woods of the Wilderness, all thick with thorn bushes, heavy grape vines, and other undergrowth. The Wilderness was so thick that the men could often barely see 20 or 30 feet (6 to 9 m) directly in front of their path, when there was a path.

The Rebels passed close by an old iron forge site called Catherine's Furnace. Their sounds in the woods drew the attention of the Union 3rd Corps, under the command of General Daniel Sickles, who believed the sounds off in the woods were a sign that Rebel forces were retreating. After receiving permission from Hooker, Sickles ordered his men forward and briefly engaged Jackson's rear guard. The fight did not last long and the Union men did not pursue the Confederates through the difficult undergrowth.

All through the day, Union troops reported to their commanders that they had heard the sounds of Rebels in the woods, but their fears were minimized. No one thought any numbers of Confederates could possibly be maneuvering through the Wilderness. Of course, they were wrong. Late in the afternoon, around 5:00 P.M., Jackson and his men had arrived just east of the crossroads of Brock Road and Orange Turnpike, just out of sight of Hooker's right. The Union men in front of him were of the 6th Corps, under the command of Major General Oliver O. Howard, who had never before led an entire corps in battle. Throughout the day, Howard had received multiple messages from Hooker, first calling on him to establish a defense line, then another ordering him to take the offensive and pursue the enemy. Howard had not only failed to move, but he had also not secured his flank, which was the farthest westward extension of Hooker's lines.

Just as the men of the 6th, many of them German immigrant troops, were sitting down to prepare their evening meal and boil their coffee, deer and other forest animals came bounding out of the nearby woods. The Federals grabbed their guns to kill some fresh meat, only to face Jackson's men emerging behind the wild animals, their clothes ragged from the thickets and brambles of the day's march. They completely surprised the Union men, and Hooker's right flank simply fell apart. Ward offers a description of the fight from one Union soldier: "It was a perfect whirlwind of men. The enemy seemed to come from every direction."

"I HAVE LOST MY RIGHT"

The fighting continued as twilight began to fall. The 6th had not only abandoned their positions, but Jackson had also managed to push them back 3 miles (5 km). As darkness fell, Jackson wanted to continue with a night engagement, which almost never took place during the Civil War. But he was talked out of it. Instead, under cover of darkness, General Jackson and his staff rode ahead of his men on horseback to examine Union positions along their new right flank, located just west of Chancellorsville.

Jackson and his men, in the confusion and the darkness, rode close to some Confederate troops, who opened fire on the general and his staffers. They wounded Jackson twice, as well as several of the officers under his command. Jackson was thrown from his horse and had to be carried off the field. His left arm was shattered, and it was amputated the following morning. General Stuart was given command of Jackson's forces. It would be the last time Stonewall Jackson would engage in a fight. He died eight days later of pneumonia. It was a dreadful loss for Lee. As noted by historian Geoffrey Ward, Lee said: "He has lost his left arm, but I have lost my right."

Jackson's march had successfully caused the rollback of Hooker's right flank. But in doing so, Hooker had become aware that Lee had divided his men. By the morning of May 3, the possibilities for the Union commander looked promising. If he could only take advantage of Lee's divided positions, he could possibly bring down the Army of Northern Virginia. But Hooker did not make obvious moves, and instead, he remained on the defensive. The night before, General Sickles had pulled back closer to Chancellorsville. By doing so, he had abandoned

The Battle of Chancellorsville (above) was a victory for the Confederate Army, but they suffered a major blow when General Stonewall Jackson was mistakenly shot by fellow soldiers. The Southern general was an important leader in the Confederate offensive attack, but he needed immediate medical attention for his injuries. Jackson's arm, shattered by friendly fire, was amputated, and he died eight days later from pneumonia.

Hazel Grove, which stood on the high ground of the battlefield. Confederates soon put up artillery units there and began to pound Chancellorsville with shot and shell. One artillery shell struck the Chancellor mansion's front porch, which caused a large chunk of plaster to fall and strike Hooker on the head. Although he was not killed, he became disoriented and was semiconscious. Nevertheless, Hooker refused to give up direct command and tried to continue directing the battle. He managed to pull his men back into a tighter formation between the rivers, with his right flank next to the Rapidan and his left on the Rappahannock. But he did not take the offensive.

As Confederate shelling continued, a shell exploded on the Chancellor mansion, setting it on fire. Other explosions set fire to the surrounding woods in several places. At the same time, the Union's Major General John Sedgwick was moving his forces from Fredericksburg after receiving a call for help from General Hooker. After several assaults, Sedgwick's men managed to get Confederate commander Jubal Early's men off of Marye's Heights, something Burnside had not been able to do five months earlier. They then marched onward to Chancellorsville. With Hooker almost bottled up, Lee turned on Sedgwick's army and nearly surrounded the Union commander. Sedgwick managed to escape Lee's clutches by moving to the north bank of the Rappahannock. Then, just as Lee was preparing to attack Hooker's defensive lines, Hooker pulled Sedgwick's forces back across the two rivers to a safer area. The Battle of Chancellorsville was over and Lee and Jackson had proven themselves to be a great pair of commanders. But it was the end for Jackson, who died of pneumonia on May 10.

Hooker had entered the Chancellorsville fight with all the confidence of a commander certain of victory. But Lee had beaten him badly. The Confederate general's actions that day were a military masterpiece, though one that came at a high cost. The casualties at Chancellorsville mounted to nearly 30,000, with the North losing 17,287 to 12,764 for the Confederates. Man for man, Lee suffered a greater percentage of casualties than Hooker, losing nearly a quarter of his army. The Army of Northern Virginia was slowly fading away.

By May 6, the Union forces had crossed back over the Rappahannock and were back where they had started before Hooker had launched his complicated and overconfident strategy. One Federal private summed up his disappointment at Hooker's failure, as noted by historian Geoffrey Ward: "Thus ended the campaign which Hooker opened as with a thunderbolt from the hand of Mars, and ended as impotently as an infant who has not learned to grasp its rattle." As for President Lincoln, who had expressed concern toward Hooker's overconfidence, he was crushed. Receiving the news of his army's great loss at Chancellorsville, Lincoln could only cry, notes historian Ward, "My God! My God! What will the country say?"

Gettysburg

The town of Gettysburg was home to 2,400 citizens in the summer of 1863. It was the center of a web of 10 intersecting roads, a pair of which led toward South Mountain 10 miles (16 km) to the west. Other local roads ran to Harrisburg and Baltimore and several other communities in Pennsylvania and Maryland. Surrounding the town were well-cultivated farms and orchards, stretching across rolling hills and ridges and occasional granite outcroppings. In some ways, the terrain was designed for a Civil War battle since the region's hills and ridges were perfect for establishing defensive positions for the army that might take control of the rolling landscape first.

CONVERGING ARMIES

Despite having a landscape designed for battle, Gettysburg was not a site chosen ahead of time by either of the two armies that would take up arms there. Following his brilliant and bold victory at Chancellorsville in early May, Robert E. Lee was determined to take the war, once again, onto Northern territory.

With Union spirits low, Lee felt that, if he won battles on Northern soil, supporters of the Union might be driven to sue for peace and end the bloody war. To Lee and to President Davis, the march to the North was a gamble worth taking. Davis gave his blessing to the plan by mid-May, and Lee was ready to move northward by June 3. Through the following days, Lee's forces, numbering about 75,000 men, marched along the south bank of the Rappahannock to the Blue Ridge.

By late June, neither Union nor Confederate forces could pinpoint their enemy's location. Then, on June 28, Lee was surprised to learn not only that the new Union commander was Major General George G. Meade, but that his army of 95,000 men had already crossed the Potomac and might be within striking distance soon. (Meade himself had actually taken up positions at Pipe Creek over in Maryland.) Lee ordered his men to begin concentrating east of the hills in the Gettysburg-Cashtown region. This was not a cautious order, since Lee had spread his lines too far apart from their advance positions to their rear, a distance of almost 100 miles (160 km). Bringing his forces together would take a little time.

On July 1, Lee ordered General A.P. Hill to send two divisions into Gettysburg to test the strength of Union forces that had been spotted in the area. By midmorning, one of Hill's division commanders, Major General Henry Heth, and his men bumped into Union cavalry just west of Gettysburg. The Union forces were under the command of Brigadier General John Buford. The Union horsemen were holding the local roads, even as they protected Gettysburg from Confederate advance. The Confederates formed together in a hurry on Herr Ridge and moved forward, attacking the Federals first on McPherson's Ridge.

JULY 1, 1863

The engagement was sharp and at close range, lasting several hours. The Union cavalrymen were pushed back toward

Gettysburg, but Buford's men, who had been fighting mostly on foot, took a stand along McPherson's Ridge. Then, just as General Heth was ready to launch an all-out attack with a pair of Rebel brigades, the Union soldiers reached the scene all at once and drove the Confederates back. The battle ended with the retreat of the Rebels from the field and the capture of the Confederates' Brigadier General James J. Archer.

At the opening of the action, both sides had sent messengers to inform their larger armies of the enemy's presence. By mid-afternoon, nearly 40,000 men were present on the field northwest of Gettysburg. Then, Confederate lieutenant general Richard S. Ewell's men attacked the Union 11th Corps, under the command of Major General Oliver Howard. The Confederates outnumbered the Yankees this time, and they pushed the Federals back to Cemetery Hill, south of the Pennsylvania town. Here, major generals Howard and Winfield S. Hancock reorganized their men to take their stand, even as they sent other forces east to occupy Culp's Hill. These positions were important, as both the South and North knew. Cemetery Hill and Culp's Hill were the high ground south of Gettysburg. If there were to be a larger fight over the next several days, these were the best positions. Despite the late hour of the day, some of the officers under Ewell's command wanted to continue the attack and try to dislodge the Federals from Cemetery Hill. But Ewell chose not to. His decision may have cost the Confederates the victory at Gettysburg.

Throughout the day, Lee and Meade rushed their forces forward to the new battlefield. Late in the day, Lee had enough forces in position to launch another attack, which he decided against doing. He had moved during the day to place his new headquarters where the Chambersburg Pike crosses Seminary Ridge, just to the west of Gettysburg. His 3rd Corps had not seen action that day, and Lee might have sent them forward toward Seminary Ridge, where they probably could have removed the thinly spread Union force. He hesitated, however, since he had not heard back from General Stuart and his cavalry. Lee had entered a battle without a key tool he generally expected to have: information about the positions and strength of his enemy. With Stuart still out in the field somewhere, the Confederate general had been fighting blind.

JULY 2, 1863

By the morning of July 2, both armies were in position along Culp's Hill and Cemetery Hill. Lee's men had no choice but to attack directly against the Federal line. Meade, who had been in command of the Army of the Potomac for only five days, knew the importance of the battle that would soon stretch up and down his defense lines. He put out an order to the soldiers under his command, as noted by historian Geoffrey Ward: "Corps and other commanders are authorized to order the instant death of any soldier who fails in his duty at this hour."

Lee was determined to make his attack against the Northern line because of his limited success of the previous day. Lee's battle plan was to send forward his most experienced officer, Lieutenant General James Longstreet of the 1st Corps, in command of the divisions of major generals John Hood and LaFayette McLaws of his corps. He also meant to send in Major General Richard Anderson's division, which was part of the 3rd Corps. The plan was to assault the Union left flank.

Unfortunately for Lee, he was wrong about the position of the Union. It was the fault of poor spying information. He thought the main Union positions were along Emmitsburg Road, instead of Cemetery Ridge. His source for this poor information was Captain Sam Johnston, the army's chief engineer, whom Lee had sent out that morning. Johnston and his unit returned to Lee around 8:30 that morning and reported that the Union line did not extend very far to the south. Lee ordered Longstreet to deliver his men across the road beyond the Union left flank and push against it hard. At the same time, General

General George Meade (center, with beard) *replaced Hooker after the devastating Union loss at the Battle of Chancellorsville. As the new commanding officer of the Federal Army, Meade set out to find and destroy General Robert E. Lee's forces. North and South would meet in a climactic battle at Gettysburg.*

Ewell's corps was to deliver a second punch against the Federal right flank at Culp's Hill.

Lee and Longstreet did not agree on whether the battle should unfold at all, given the superior positions of the Union side. Longstreet thought they should leave and let Meade pursue the Confederates until they found a field position that was to their advantage. But Lee, sick with repeating bouts of dysentery and tired of the war in general, would not listen. According to historian Edwin Bearss, he told his right-hand general: "The enemy is there, and I am going to attack him." Longstreet responded: "If he is there in the morning that means he wants you to attack him—a good reason for not doing so." Lee's reply was steadfast, even stubborn: "I am going to whip them, or they are going to whip me." The Battle of Gettysburg was one fought by choice for Lee. It would prove to be one of his worst decisions of the war.

Longstreet had some delays that morning that remain controversial even today. It was past noon by the time he had moved his men forward. In the meantime, General Stuart finally arrived, having been away from Lee for more than a week. Lee was angry with Stuart, telling him, as recalled by historian Ward: "I have not heard from you for days, and you the eyes and ears of my army." Stuart could only inform Lee that he had captured 125 Union wagons and their teams, to which Lee responded: "Yes, and they are an impediment to me now."

As the Confederates prepared to attack, a general along the Union line changed his position. Major General Daniel E. Sickles was assigned to hold the Union left against Longstreet's 3rd Corps along the lower end of Cemetery Ridge and Little Round Top. Against orders from Meade, Sickles moved his men forward, a grave mistake. By pushing forward and out of position, he could not mount a strong defense.

With Longstreet's men finally on the march, it was Meade's chief engineer, Major General Gouverneur K. Warren, who realized that Sickles had left his position on Little Round Top. He and a young lieutenant named Washington Roebling, who would one day design the Brooklyn Bridge, reached the unprotected hill. However, they found only signalmen in position there. Warren quickly sent a brigade of the 5th Corps to hold the rock outcropping. By now, Sickles and his men were under fire, pinned down in the Peach Orchard. According to historian Geoffrey Ward, Roebling later remembered: "One glance sufficed to note the head of Hood's Texans coming up the rocky ravine which separates Little and Big Round Top. I ran down, told General Warren, he came up with me and saw the necessity of immediate action."

It was then that General Warren ordered Colonel Joshua Lawrence Chamberlain and his 20th Maine to secure the peak of Little Round Top. With only minutes to spare, Chamberlain and his few hundred troops scrambled up the hill and spent the following hours fighting, vastly outnumbered. Chamberlain ordered the men on his left to fall back and form again at a right angle to the remainder of his regiment, all the time firing their guns. As noted by historian Geoffrey Ward, one of Chamberlain's men, Private Gerrish, later wrote: "Imagine, if you can, nine small companies of infantry, numbering perhaps three hundred men, in the form of a right angle, on the extreme flank of an army of eighty thousand men, put there to hold the key of the entire position against a force at least ten times their number. . . . Stand firm, ye boys from Maine."

The fight raged on, with the Alabama men pushing the Maine men from their hilltop positions five times, only to have Chamberlain's men fight their way back to the top again. The fighting was extremely close, so close a man could almost reach out and touch his opponent. After a prolonged engagement, the men of the 20th Maine reached into their cartridge boxes and found little left. A desperate Chamberlain ordered his men to fix bayonets and charge down the hill. They caught the Confederates by surprise. Many Rebels turned and ran, while others surrendered immediately.

THE VALLEY OF DEATH

Sickles and his men fought furiously, but Sickles paid for his error in judgment when a Confederate cannonball struck him and destroyed his right leg. As noted by historian Ward, a Union captain saw it all:

> I was within a few feet of General Sickles when he received the wound by which he lost his leg. A terrific explosion

seemed to shake the very earth . . . instantly followed by another. I . . . noticed that [his] pants and drawers at the knee were torn clear off to the leg, which was swinging loose. . . . He was carried from the field, coolly smoking a cigar.

Sickles's corps was nearly destroyed by Longstreet's men. By the time the battle ended that evening, the Federals still held the field. They had, however, been pushed back to their original positions along Cemetery Ridge and Little Round Top, where Meade had placed them earlier in the day. The fighting in the orchard, out in the Wheatfield, at Devil's Den, and at a site called the Valley of Death was some of the most ferocious of the battle. One Confederate Texan claimed there were so many bullets in the air that one could have held up his cap and filled it. According to historian Ward, a Massachusetts private referred to the battle as "a perfect hell on earth, never, perhaps to be equaled, certainly not to be surpassed, nor *ever* to be forgotten in a man's lifetime."

About a mile to the north of the Peach Orchard and the Wheatfield, another unit of Alabama troops broke a hold in the Cemetery Ridge line, close to its center. The gap had been created by Sickles's unapproved advance into the orchard earlier in the day. Here, the line was in the hands of General Winfield Scott Hancock's 2nd Corps. At that point in the line, however, Hancock had only eight companies of one regiment available to immediately meet the Confederate breakthrough. These men belonged to the 1st Minnesota, which had participated in every major battle of the war to that date since First Bull Run.

The 1st Minnesota numbered only 262, but they were all Hancock had, so he ordered them forward into the face of 1,600 Alabamians. He gave them orders to slow the enemy down to provide time for reinforcements to arrive. The Minnesota men moved quickly, fixing bayonets and charging down the hill into the mouth of the enemy. They forced the Confederates back, but at an extraordinary cost. Only 47 of the Minnesotans survived their counterattack without being wounded or killed. That is an 82 percent casualty rate, which took place in less than five minutes. Historian Geoffrey Ward notes that their losses were "the highest percentage of casualties taken by any Union regiment in the war."

Elsewhere along the Union line of defense, the fighting had unfolded less intensely than on the Union left flank. Lee had ordered Ewell to advance toward Culp's Hill on the Union right, but his men had accomplished little. Near the end of the day, a division of Ewell's 2nd Corps, Major General Edward Johnson's division, did move against Culp's Hill. Meade had only earlier ordered Major General Henry W. Slocum's 12th Corps off the hill to provide support for his left flank. But Slocum had asked to keep one brigade in position on Culp's Hill. It was that brigade that held the hill against Ewell's men until the shroud of darkness brought an end to the fighting there. Even after nightfall, Major General Early's Confederate division of Ewell's 2nd Corps launched an attack on Cemetery Hill and managed to reach Federal positions before they were pushed back. Two days of fighting had taken place, and Meade was still in control of Cemetery Ridge, Culp's Hill, and the two Round Tops. The day ended with each side having suffered about 9,000 casualties, bringing the total for two days of fighting to almost 35,000.

THE FINAL DAY

During the night of July 2 to 3, General Slocum returned with his 12th Corps (minus one brigade that had been left behind) to Culp's Hill only to find General Johnson's division of the 2nd Corps hugging the southeastern rim of the hill. The 12th was determined to drive off the Rebels. At 4:30 in the morning on July 3, Union artillery opened up on the Confederates. But 15 minutes later, the Rebels were attacking up Culp's Hill. The

General Daniel E. Sickles (center) *lost his leg during the Battle of Gettysburg. The damaged bone was later sent to the Army Medical Museum in Washington, D.C., accompanied by a note: "With compliments of Major General D.E.S." Sickles would continue to visit his leg in the museum for years to come.*

assault went on for the next five hours, but it ended in failure for the Confederates, who did not manage to remove the Federals.

While the Confederates were attacking Culp's Hill, Lee hoped to move most of his troops to his own center, having tried to remove the Union men from both their flanks the previous day. He ordered Longstreet to manage the attack. Once again, Longstreet did not cooperate.

According to Lee's plan, the infantry assault was to be preceded by a massive artillery barrage designed to soften up the enemy. He hoped that cannon fire would crush the Union center, leaving that portion of the line weak in the face of a massive attack. He ordered 164 cannons lined up opposite the Federal center and placed them under the command of the 1st Corps artillery commander, Colonel E. Porter Alexander. Lee let Alexander decide whether an infantry attack should follow his artillery barrage. But the artillery commander knew that he only had enough ammunition for a single, full-scale bombardment, after which there would be no more shells. This meant that the infantry would have to be sent forward regardless.

At 1:07 P.M. on July 3, Alexander ordered his gunners to open fire. For the following 45 minutes, according to historian Steven Woodworth, Confederate guns created "the heaviest artillery bombardment ever heard on the North American continent." In the meantime, Union gunners held their fire to conserve ammunition. Unfortunately for the Confederates, much of Alexander's artillery barrage did not accomplish its goals. As the cannons were fired again and again, the repeated rocking of their wheels created ruts that caused the artillery to overshoot their targets. As a result, many shells landed harmlessly in back of the Union center.

Union cannons eventually answered the Rebel shot and shell. As many as 80 Federal guns were fired in response to the Confederate barrage, but the Yankee artillery units held back. They sometimes waited 15 minutes between barrages to keep saving shot. When the Union guns were fired, they were more deadly than the Confederates'. Several Federal cannons were not used at all but instead were held back to use against the Rebel assault that was certain to come. After half an hour of firing, the Union chief of artillery, Brigadier General Henry J. Hunt, ordered all his guns silenced. He hoped to convince the Rebels that their artillery attack had hit their marks. It was then that General Alexander told General George Pickett that it was the moment for the infantry assault.

Then, about 13,000 Confederate infantry began marching out of the woods toward the Union center, which lay 1,200 yards (1 km) in the distance. There was nothing but gently sloping and open ground between the two lines. As the Union men watched the Confederates moving bravely in unison across the field, they could not help but be impressed. All three divisions marched toward the Union center.

During the first 900 yards (820 m) of the Rebel march, long-range Union artillery on both flanks opened up, causing moderate casualties. In front of the Confederates, the Federal guns remained silent to help lure the enemy forward. Their cannons were loaded with short-range canister shot. At about 240 yards (220 m) from the Union line, Emmitsburg Road cut the field in front of the advancing Rebels at an angle. In several places along the road, the Confederates reached zigzag wooden fences that they had to climb over.

At that moment, the short-range cannons finally opened fire, delivering a wall of leaden death. Rebel troops began to fall in large numbers. At 200 yards (180 m), infantry units, including those from Vermont, Ohio, and New York, opened up on the Rebels. Several of Pickett's troops continued to advance and actually managed to reach the low stone wall that was protecting Union troops in the center of their line. But as they arrived at the wall, they were pushed back. One Confederate officer, General Lewis A. Armistead, managed to break the Union line and place his hand on the barrel of a Yankee cannon, but he was then shot down.

What became known as Pickett's Charge ended in absolute disaster. Of the 13,000 Confederates who had marched across the open ground toward the Union center, barely half of them returned to their comrades' lines. Pickett lost 2 out of every 3 of his men. Three of his brigadier generals and all 13 of his colonels were either killed or wounded. Those who managed to stumble back to their lines were met by General Lee on his horse, riding back and forth in their path. According to historian James McPherson, he told his men, "It's all my fault. It is I who have lost this fight, and you must help me out of it the best way you can. All good men must rally." Some did rally, as Lee

Hoping to demoralize Union forces, General Robert E. Lee led his men into the Battle of Gettysburg. After two days of intense fighting, however, the South began to lose ground and Lee ordered one final push against the Union front. This desperate maneuver, known as Pickett's Charge (above), was one of the most devastating military orders of the Civil War.

and Longstreet prepared for the counterattack they believed Meade would launch at their weakened center.

But Meade did not attack. The general had been in command for only six days, and he could not make himself order an attack. He was uncertain just how severely damaged the Rebels in front of him actually were. Lee was beaten. On July 2, Lee had attacked the Union flanks and failed, and on the afternoon of July 3, striking at the Union middle, the results were the same.

Across the North, news of the victory at Gettysburg was delivered up and down the nation's telegraph lines. But the victory at Gettysburg came at a high cost of manpower. Through three days of fighting, more than 50,000 casualties had fallen, including 23,000 on the Union side and 28,000 among the Rebels. The Southern forces had not only taken higher casualties by number and as a percentage of their total number of men, but lost soldiers were also becoming increasingly difficult to replace. From the beginning, the Civil War had always been a fight in which available men slowly shrank in number. The South had a limited number of men to draw from for its armies. By the summer of 1863, a gap was widening to the point of breaking: It was the gap between the number of troops the Confederacy needed to continue its fight against the Yankees and the number of men actually available.

Chattanooga

ee had failed at Gettysburg. The battle was costly for the
Confederacy, and it was celebrated across the North. Another major Union victory came directly on its heels. Farther to the west, General Ulysses S. Grant had surrounded the
Mississippi River town of Vicksburg, one of the last Rebel hold-
outs on the great river. For six weeks, Grant had bottled up its
citizens, plus a Confederate force of 20,000, and nearly starved
out the population. Then, on July 4, the day after Meade's victory at Gettysburg, General John C. Pemberton surrendered his
forces and Vicksburg fell into Northern hands. Complete Union
control of the Mississippi River soon became reality.

ROSECRANS AND BRAGG

In other action in the West, two large-scale armies had been
locked in combat over and over again throughout 1863. The
Union forces under General William S. Rosecrans and Confederate forces under General Braxton Bragg had first fought
in a two-day battle that began on December 31 and ended on

January 1, 1863. The fight took place between 44,000 Union troops and 35,000 Rebels at Murfreesboro, Tennessee (remembered also as the Battle of Stones River). It resulted in Bragg's defeat, but he withdrew his forces to fight another day.

Both armies slipped into winter quarters following the fight at Murfreesboro. With the arrival of spring, Rosecrans received orders from Washington to begin moving against the enemy. Although his army numbered 75,000 by then, he refused to move. In George McClellan fashion, he instead demanded more men, supplies, and horses.

In the meantime, Bragg and his 40,000 men watched the Union Army closely. By June, Rosecrans was ready to fight. The two armies jabbed at each other for several days from late June to early July. Rosecrans forced Bragg to abandon his base at Tullahoma, Tennessee, and retreat to Chattanooga, on the border between West Tennessee and Georgia. They were reinforced there by an additional 20,000-man army. By mid-August, Rosecrans was on the march toward Chattanooga. Over the following three weeks, he had crossed his entire army over the Tennessee River, forcing Bragg and his small force to abandon Chattanooga.

As Bragg's army retreated southward, Rosecrans attacked on September 9, sending three corps against the enemy. However, his three units marched so far apart that 40 miles (64 km) of the rugged Tennessee Mountains eventually separated them. Believing he had Bragg on the run, Rosecrans pushed his men forward. Bragg then took the offensive on September 10, knowing that Rosecrans's armies were greatly separated. The assault against Union major general George Thomas's corps was unsuccessful. Two days later, Bragg attacked again, this time against Major General Thomas Crittenden. Again, the Confederate attack failed.

"THE ROCK OF CHICKAMAUGA"

Then, Bragg began receiving reinforcements from the East, as Lee had sent Longstreet with 12,000 men out to Tennessee. By

September 18, 7,000 of Longstreet's men had reached Bragg's army, in time to participate in the Battle of Chickamauga. When the battle opened on the morning of September 19, General Thomas, who thought he was sending his men against a Confederate infantry brigade, discovered too late that the enemy was actually cavalry forces under General Nathan Bedford Forrest. The battle lines spread out quickly, and by mid-afternoon, the fight was on along the entire length of the Federal line. The day was a seesaw of action, as neither side gained an ultimate break along the 6 miles (10 km) of the front.

That evening, General Longstreet himself arrived. He and Bragg divided their forces into two wings, with Longstreet taking command of the left flank. As fighting opened the following day, General Rosecrans made a great mistake when he moved forces along the line to fill a gap he thought was along his left flank. By doing so, he created a large gap along his right flank. At 11:00 A.M., the battle not yet two hours old, Longstreet saw Rosecrans's error and poured 11,000 men in the breach, causing Rosecrans's right flank to fall apart. General George Thomas was only able to drive back the Rebels because Bragg did not follow up on Longstreet's move. Thomas's efforts gained him the nickname of the "Rock of Chickamauga." He organized an orderly retreat, saving Rosecrans's army.

Following their defeat at Chickamauga, September 19 to 20, Federal forces took refuge in the city of Chattanooga. They soon found themselves trapped. Braxton Bragg's Army of Tennessee, a total of 60,000 men, occupied the high ground of Lookout Mountain to the southwest and Missionary Ridge to the east. (Rosecrans made a great mistake when he ordered his men to abandon Lookout Mountain on September 24, giving the Confederates the opportunity to take it.) Additional Confederate forces managed to block Union supply lines, and it looked as if the Yankees might be slowly starved to death, if Rosecrans chose not to surrender. There was a supply line to Chattanooga—the Wagon Road through the mountains that

After the Battle of Gettysburg, Union forces gained more ground following several hard-won victories in other Southern states. In Tennessee, for example, Union general William S. Rosencrans unwisely gave up Lookout Mountain (above) to the Confederates, a mistake that gave General Ulysses S. Grant command of Union soldiers.

crosses Walden's Ridge through Anderson's Crossroads and into nearby Bridgeport—but Confederates harassed this route constantly. Also, when heavy rains set in, the ground was miserable to cross. Food became so scarce for Rosecrans's army that thousands of Union horses were killed and eaten.

GRANT TO THE RESCUE

From distant Washington, D.C., President Lincoln observed Rosecrans's situation with disappointment and disgust. His commander did not seem up to the task of command. Lincoln famously referred to Rosecrans, as noted by historian Tyler Dennett, as "confused and stunned like a duck hit on the head." Lincoln ordered a shake-up of commands, uniting the departments of the Ohio, Cumberland, and the Tennessee into the Military Division of the Mississippi. He then relieved Rosecrans and placed Ulysses S. Grant in command. Since Grant's orders from Lincoln gave him the authority to sack Rosecrans, the new commander wasted no time doing so. Already, General Halleck had sent General Sherman with four divisions from Vicksburg to Chattanooga, but he had to rebuild the railroad line along the way, slowing down Sherman's men for weeks. Secretary of War Edwin Stanton then asked Lincoln to transfer the 11th and 12th Corps by train from the Army of the Potomac out to help with Rosecrans's situation. Lincoln agreed and activated Joseph Hooker to command them.

Stanton then called several railroad presidents to Washington to discuss how to quickly deliver thousands of Union troops to Chattanooga. Less than 48 hours after the meeting, Federal forces were on their way to Tennessee, with Chattanooga more than 1,200 miles (1,900 km) away. Within two weeks, 20,000 Union troops had reached the railhead near Chattanooga, along with artillery, horses, and tons of equipment. Historian James McPherson referred to this move of forces across the country as "the longest and fastest movement of such a large body of troops before the twentieth century." The rescue of Rosecrans's army was in action.

Grant reached Chattanooga by October 23 and ordered the opening of a new supply route called the Cracker Line. It fell to the 11th Corps—which had been beaten so badly at Chancellorsville and suffered greatly at Gettysburg—to open the supply route. The unit fought well during a night skirmish on October 28 to 29, which helped them gain confidence and regain some face. With Grant on the scene, many Federals had a confidence they had not had with Rosecrans. Historian Bruce Catton notes the feelings expressed by one Union officer, who thought, after Grant's arrival, "we began to see things move. We felt that everything came from a plan." Ironically, Rosecrans's staff had actually been the planners of much of the operation that unfolded after Grant reached Chattanooga.

Things were, indeed, moving. Confederate forces could do little but watch. Sherman arrived with his 17,000 men of the Army of the Tennessee, which were added to the 20,000 Hooker had delivered from the Army of the Potomac. General Thomas had been on the scene from the beginning with his 35,000-man Army of the Cumberland.

Bragg's possibilities were shrinking. He still held the high ground on Lookout Mountain and Missionary Ridge, but he was facing increasing numbers of Federals and disagreement and rebellion among his own side. He blamed the officers under his command for the failures during the Chickamauga battle. He suspended General Leonidas Polk and a pair of other generals, raising the anger of General Nathan Bedford Forrest, who declared he would no longer serve under Bragg. Other generals sent around a petition calling for Bragg's removal. Anger among the Confederate commanders grew so intense that President Davis took a special train on October 6 and made his way to Chattanooga to meet with Bragg and his officers.

In the end, Davis just moved several of Bragg's generals to other battle areas and sent Longstreet off to Knoxville,

Tennessee, to try and recapture the city. Longstreet's mission ultimately failed. Bragg kept his command, Davis left, and few Confederates were any happier than they had been before President Davis's arrival.

Once Longstreet and his 15,000 men left Bragg, there was no possible way for the Confederates to keep their positions in

Life of the Common Soldier

While generals find their way into history books, it is important to remember that common soldiers, often volunteers, are the ones who fight the war. Before the Civil War, they had been farmers, shop clerks, factory workers, dockhands—even college professors—who had never been in combat before.

Each man entered the ranks of his respective army with his own sense of cause. Southerners fought to maintain a way of life, to support the existence and expansion of slavery, or in opposition to racial equality. Northerners fought to keep the Union intact and to keep slavery out of the western territories—a struggle that had raged before the war.

Since enlisted men lived an outdoor existence in tents, bad weather, disease, poor food, and a lack of sanitation made camp life miserable. In addition, camp life was often routine and dull. Between battles, troops often drank alcohol. Soldiers who could not afford to buy liquor would often make their own. Recipes included such ingredients as bark juice, tar-water, turpentine, sugar, and lamp oil.

Homesickness was a constant pull for many soldiers farther from home than they had ever been. Soldiers became even more nostalgic for home when they listened to the popular music found in the camps. Such sentimental songs as "Weeping Sad and Lonely," "The Vacant Chair," and others expressed emotional longings that never went away.

the field much longer. The initiative for the coming battle automatically fell to General Grant. Grant had in mind a strategy that went beyond the simple freeing of the troops from Chattanooga. Once the Confederates were removed from the region, he then wanted to follow up with a march into Georgia. The future direction of the war in the western battle areas depended on what might happen next at Chattanooga.

THE BATTLE ABOVE THE CLOUDS

It was clear to the Union leaders that the Confederates would need to be driven from their high ground positions. Grant rejected any suggestion to send men toward Missionary Ridge in a direct frontal assault. At the base of the ridge, the Rebels were well dug in, situated in three lines of trenches or rifle pits. Instead, Grant ordered attacks on both the Confederate flanks, sending Sherman toward the enemy's left and Hooker to the right to storm Lookout Mountain. The mountain commanded the landscape at 1,600 feet (490 m) in height above the Tennessee River. At his center, he placed General Thomas's Army of the Cumberland. Grant was uncertain these men had the capacity to mount a serious attack. After all, they had been beaten soundly at Chickamauga and now needed to be rescued. According to historian James McPherson, Grant thought Thomas's men "could not be got out of their trenches to assume the offensive." He would soon be proven wrong. By placing the veterans of Chickamauga in such a secondary role, Grant may have been unknowingly challenging them to prove themselves once more in battle.

As the Union forces began to move against the Confederates on the higher elevations, they met with success and failure. Hooker moved brilliantly, moving his three divisions on November 24 against three Confederate brigades in command of the northern slope of Lookout Mountain. As the Union men moved awkwardly up the mountain, amid scatters of large

Grant shrewdly reduced the role of General George Thomas's men, the recently defeated Union soldiers from the Battle of Chickamauga, as a subtle reminder of their failure. When the fighting began, however, it was Thomas's men who broke the Confederate line of defense at the battle of Missionary Ridge (above).

boulders and downed trees, they reached an elevation shrouded in a thin fog. This gave the name often used in later years to describe the fighting: Battle Above the Clouds.

Ultimately taking fewer than 500 casualties, Hooker and his men drove the Confederates out of their positions and down Lookout Mountain's opposite slope. Bragg had no choice but to abandon his defenses on Lookout and pull his men back to Missionary Ridge. Through the night, once the clouds cleared out, troops on both sides were able to watch a total eclipse of the moon. By the next morning, a Union unit of volunteers from

Kentucky reached the peak of Lookout Mountain and planted a large U.S. flag, visible to both armies below.

But the fight up the mountain had taken all day on November 25. Meanwhile, on the Union left flank, Sherman faced a more difficult assault than Hooker. Lookout Mountain had proven hard to defend for the Confederates, but it was the Federals who faced challenges from the terrain. The ground was swampy and uneven and defended by one of the South's most capable division commanders, Major General Patrick R. Cleburne. Both flanks failed to accomplish their goals by mid-afternoon.

In the end, Grant sent General Thomas's men forward to make a limited assault against the first of the three rifle pits of the Confederates on Missionary Ridge. In part, Grant meant to occupy the Rebels at their center to keep Bragg from sending reinforcements to support Cleburne's lines. In all, 23,000 Union men, involving four divisions, were sent toward the ridge across a stretch of ground 2 miles (3 km) long along an open plain that led straight into the Confederate lines. For some, it looked like Pickett's Charge all over again, only with Union men exposing themselves to destruction at Rebel hands. The odds appeared even more in the South's favor, since Bragg's men had already had two months to entrench, plus Missionary Ridge lay at a higher elevation than Cemetery Ridge.

UP MISSIONARY RIDGE

The day would belong to Thomas's men, who felt they had something to prove to the other Union armies that had been sent to their rescue. Due to some confusion of orders, plus some changes made by mid-ranking officers, the men of the Army of the Cumberland quickly forced the Confederate defenders from their rifle pits, but sent them scrambling up the ridge.

Thomas's men did not stop at the bottom of the slope as Grant had ordered but kept going as a reckless direct frontal assault. Waiting at the bottom of the hill did not make sense once the Union forces turned the Rebels out of their first line of trenches. Staying there would have left them in the open and vulnerable to rifle fire higher up the ridge. So, they proceeded up the hill, by the platoon, the company, the regiment, and the brigade.

Before the Union assault by the Army of the Cumberland up Missionary Ridge was over, 60 regimental flags had advanced up the hill. In their face, a startled enemy melted away. Evening fell and stopped the Union pursuit. Almost all of Bragg's men, except for Cleburne's division, which put up a hard rear-guard defense, did not stop to regroup until they had put 30 miles (50 km) between themselves and the Yankees at Chattanooga.

The ridge that many on both sides of the fight had thought was impregnable—unable to be captured—had proven to be less so. Historian James McPherson recalls Grant's words after the assault: "Well, it *was* impregnable." The Federals took 4,000 Confederates prisoner that day. As for Bragg, he did not accept defeat for himself, choosing instead to blame his men for his loss. The Battle of Chattanooga proved to be one of the most dramatic victories of the entire war. The casualty record included 5,824 on the Union side and 6,667, including those captured, for the Confederates. Bragg would lose his command after the fight. It was Bragg who may have been the one responsible for his army's loss, considering his continued presence caused such low spirits among his men. This was true even after President Davis's visit to Tennessee. Bragg stated as much in a letter he wrote to Davis, offering to resign, as noted by historian James McDonough: "I fear we both erred in the conclusion for me to retain command here after the clamor raised against me."

Chattanooga signaled a turn of events for the Rebels. A clerk in the Confederate War Department, John B. Jones, was nearly hopeless after Bragg's loss along the banks of the Tennessee River. In his diary, Jones wrote words recalled by historian McPherson: "Unless something is done . . . we are irretrievably gone." The South's loss at Chattanooga was only heightened when Union forces pushed back an attack by Longstreet at Knoxville later that same month. Back in Virginia, Lee had failed in a small-framed campaign to turn the enemy's right flank and place his army between Meade's Army of the Potomac and Washington, D.C. Meade also failed to turn Lee's right flank along the Rapidan. Still, the South's casualties were twice that of the Federals, resulting in the loss of 4,000 men of the South, men whom Lee and the Confederacy could not afford to do without. Southerners had been filled with hope when Bragg had bottled Rosecrans inside Chattanooga early in the fall. But, as armies on both sides slipped into winter quarters, the future for the Confederacy began to look dire, indeed.

Spotsylvania

With Ulysses S. Grant's successful rescue of the stranded Union army in Chattanooga, President Lincoln made one of the best decisions of his presidency. He placed the Illinois general over all Federal troops, then moved him to the eastern theater.

Once Grant gained command of all Federal forces in early 1864, he proposed a broad-based offensive. The plan was to use the North's superior numbers of men in uniform to attack the Confederacy along several key fronts, with the intention of bringing the South down and the war to an end. He would march with Meade's army in Virginia against Robert E. Lee, which would pit these two Civil War bulldogs against one another for the first time since the first shots were fired at Fort Sumter three years earlier. In the meantime, more Union forces would advance up the James River toward Richmond, much the same way McClellan had during his campaign up Virginia's peninsula two years earlier. A third army, led by General William Tecumseh Sherman, was to move out of

Chattanooga, where it had wintered following the great battle with Bragg's army, and move southeast toward Atlanta to destroy that strategic Southern rail and manufacturing city.

GRANT AND LEE

On May 5, Grant and Meade moved against Lee. The stakes were high. Grant knew he must not only defeat Lee—a feat others, including McClellan and Meade, had already accomplished—but the Southern army had to be completely destroyed. Grant's 120,000 men would soon engage Lee's 65,000 on the same ground outside Chancellorsville where many had fought a year earlier: the Wilderness.

The fight opened in the midst of the underbrush and hanging grapevines of the Chancellorsville woods. The fight was nightmarish, as mobility and military lines were nearly impossible to establish, much less maintain. Troops got lost amid the heavy wooded growth, smoke, and fires from exploding shells and muzzle flashes. Wounded soldiers, unable to move, were burned alive by the dozens. Troops fired on their own men. After a day of back-and-forth fighting, both armies broke from the fight, with no clear winner emerging from the vine-covered battlefield.

The next day, many veterans of the Army of the Potomac expected Grant to move away from Lee's forces to lick his wounds and wait to fight another day, weeks or months later. Instead, the Federal commander sent his troops forward against Lee by moving his left flank in a movement intended to keep Lee blocked in between the Union Army and Richmond. As the outcome of the battle tipped, Lee feared defeat. Bravely, the Confederate general came forward and tried to lead troops from the front, putting himself closer than usual to the heat of the battle. His men would not allow it. As told by historian Gene Smith, Confederates virtually surrounded their commander. "Go back, General Lee. Lee to the rear." A Rebel sergeant grabbed Lee's horse reins to stop his general's advance. "Go back, General Lee,

After his victory at the Battle of Missionary Ridge, General Ulysses S. Grant was awarded command of all Union forces. Determined to crush the Confederate Army, Grant led 120,000 Union soldiers into the Wilderness against 65,000 Confederate troops in the Battle of Spotsylvania (above).

this is no place for you; we'll settle this." As Lee shouted, "Charge! Charge, boys!", his men continued their shouts: "Go back, General Lee! Go back! We won't go on unless you go back!" Lee finally withdrew from the heat of the battle.

Just as Union forces were on the brink of victory, Northern units lost their way in the thick woods. Then, Lee was reinforced by fresh troops when Longstreet's men reached the battlefield, having been absent the previous day. Throughout the rest of the day, the action seesawed back and forth with no clear winner again. After two days of fighting, Union forces had experienced 17,000 casualties. There were 11,000 casualties for the Confederates, which made for an equal percentage for both sides. But Grant was still not ready to break off the fight. His next maneuver was to move by his left flank and engage Lee at the only spot possible, given the lay of the land and the placement of roads—Spotsylvania Court House, located just a few miles from the Wilderness.

A STRATEGIC LOCATION

On the evening of May 7, Grant sent his men forward once again, by the left flank to the southeast, this time toward Spotsylvania Court House. Grant understood that the location was key and that reaching it before Lee would provide him with an advantage, given the lay of the land in the region.

Lee also understood the importance of Spotsylvania and sent his cavalry under General Jeb Stuart, and his 1st Corps, commanded by Major General Richard H. Anderson, to move as quickly as possible to occupy the small Virginia community and the nearby crossroads. He and the remainder of his army would catch up as soon as possible. This command by Lee was not as easy to accomplish as it might seem. For one thing, Confederates had to carve a road to Spotsylvania, since there was no direct route otherwise from their field position. Grant's forces, however, did have a good road to follow to Spotsylvania, but there were delays in their advance and some confusion among the divisions.

By the morning of May 8, Lee's cavalry had arrived at Spotsylvania, without a Union man in sight. But Federal cavalry arrived close by, under the command of General Phil Sheridan, before Anderson's men. Southern infantry, however, reached the small town before the Union's infantry arrived, the 5th Corps under Major General Gouverneur K. Warren. Some fighting broke out, but it was scattered and decided nothing. The real battle would have to wait, as troops from both sides arrived throughout the day and into the evening. In the meantime, both armies busied themselves digging into trenches for the fight.

On the morning of May 9, the armies were largely in place. Even before the battle unfolded, a Confederate sniper cut down the Union commander of the 6th Corps, Major General John Sedgwick. The day saw little action, however, as Grant waited until May 10 to launch several attacks against Lee's lines of defense, without managing to break through. Lee had chosen his defense lines well. Using the local terrain to his advantage, Lee had centered his line around a large, round hill that stuck out into Union territory. The hill was known as the Mule Shoe. The position was easy to defend and difficult to crack.

Grant's only partial success that day was an assault on the west side of the hill. Union colonel Emory Upton created a dense formation of 12 handpicked regiments and sent them forward with orders to not even stop and fire their guns, but to storm the enemy and keep running until they managed to breach the Confederate works. They managed to do exactly that, described by historian McPherson as "screaming like madmen and fighting like wild animals," reaching the Southern Army's first line of trenches, fanning out to the left and right to force their newly created break even wider, even as they continued toward the second line of trench works. Through this assault, the Federals managed to take 1,000 of the enemy prisoner.

Colonel Upton's men had advanced a half mile (800 m) ahead of the Union main line. But when the Rebels counterattacked, Upton's men were forced back, due in part to the failure of other Federal forces to move forward and back them up. Those assigned to provide support for Upton attacked only half-heartedly and ran in the face of massed artillery.

Still, Colonel Upton's strategy had worked, a success noted by General Grant, who decided to try the same tactic, but on a much grander scale. (Upton himself received a battlefield promotion.) It required so much planning and reworking of Union units that Grant and his officers spent all of May 11 planning. Rain fell most of that day, and they intended to launch the massive Union assault the next morning.

At the same time, Grant sent Sheridan and his cavalry on a long-distance raid behind Lee's lines, driving to the very outskirts of Richmond. There, Stuart's cavalry finally caught up with the mounted blues, leading to a fight at Yellow Tavern, just 5 miles (8 km) north of the Confederate capital. The fighting might have had no result, except for the death of one Confederate cavalryman—Jeb Stuart—who was cut down by a Union bullet. Sheridan continued to fight outside Richmond until he reached Union infantry under the command of Major General Benjamin Butler, who was positioned at Bermuda Hundred.

A SURPRISED LEE

When Grant launched his massive and creative assault on the morning of May 12, he caught Lee by surprise. The Confederate commander incorrectly expected that Grant would move by his left flank to the southeast and avoid a direct fight. Instead, the Union general sent General Winfield Scott Hancock's men, the entire 2nd Corps, toward the center of the Mule Shoe in an attack that opened well before dawn. To meet Grant where he expected him to move, Lee had ordered Lieutenant General Richard S. Ewell's forces to abandon the Mule Shoe. In fact, Ewell's artillery forces of 22 cannons had already been pulled out of the Mule Shoe before Grant's attack. By the time Lee figured out his mistake, 15,000 Federal troops were overrunning the Confederate center, and Ewell's cannons could not be sent back toward the Mule Shoe in time. Instead, Grant's men captured all of these artillery pieces. In addition, Union forces captured a division and its commander, Major General Edward Johnson. Both had earlier served under Stonewall Jackson.

Hancock's 2nd Corps had managed to divide Lee's forces in two. Lee pushed a reserve division to the front of the fight and desperately tried to lead their charge himself. He had been drawn to the same thing six days earlier during the fighting in the Wilderness.

And fight they did. The Confederates launched a counterattack that was furious and successful, in part, due to the earlier advances in the field by Yankee units. The Union advances had left the North's lines broken up and separated groups of Federals from one another. The Northern forces had advanced in rain and had become disorganized. Confederates pushed them back to the toe of the Mule Shoe, and Grant's men fell into the trench lines they had just earlier captured.

Here, Grant ordered Warren's 5th Corps and the 9th Corps, commanded by Major General Ambrose Burnside to push hard against the Confederates along the Mule Shoe by attacking on both the enemy's right and left flanks. As both corps drove forward, Hancock's 6th Corps moved against the Confederates as well. For the next 20 hours, beginning that morning and lasting until midnight, the fight raged, as North and South, according to historian Steven Woodworth, "remained at close range, shooting, bayoneting, clubbing, and grabbling each other hand-to-hand." The action was centered along trench lines that were separated by only a few hundred yards. The fighting was so close, the two armies so overlapped on the field, that, as historian Joseph P. Cullen quotes a member of the Union 6th Corps: "The flags of both armies waved at the same moment over the same breastworks while beneath them Federal and Confederate endeavored to drive home the bayonet through the interstices [small cracks] of the logs."

Nowhere was the fighting more intense than at a point in the Confederate trench lines where the lines bent, a spot that would later be called the Bloody Angle. Here, men jumped on small mounds of earth and fired their muskets down on enemy troops, only to launch their empty bayoneted guns down like spears. They then were handed other guns to repeat their actions. The fighting along Bloody Angle was so fierce that, according to

Union general Ulysses S. Grant, a war hero and veteran of the Mexican-American War, was one of the most brilliant military figures of the Civil War. Although he had made several mistakes when leading Union forces against the Confederacy, Grant's triumphant victories at Vicksburg and Chattanooga led to President Abraham Lincoln's refusal to remove Grant from leadership.

McPherson, "at one point just behind the southern lines an oak tree nearly two feet thick was cut down by minie balls." (The stump of this alleged tree was put on display more than a decade after the war at the Centennial Exposition in Philadelphia and was then sent to the Smithsonian Institution for preservation.) Throughout the fighting, however, the Confederates held on. Both Union commanders—Burnside and Warren—failed to punch through the enemy line.

THE MULE SHOE

By the early hours of May 13, General Lee managed to complete a defensive line that stretched across the base of the Mule Shoe.

He then ordered General Ewell's 2nd Corps to move back to that position. May 12 had proven a terrible day of fighting for both sides. The Union casualties alone were 6,800 men, and the Confederates lost 9,000 of their own. At the Bloody Angle, the ground and the trenches were littered with corpses. According to McPherson, "Union soldiers on a burial detail found 150 dead Southerners piled several deep in one area of trench measuring 200 square feet (18.5 square meters), and buried them by simply pushing in the parapet [a mound of dirt] on top of them."

Grant had already set his course of action for his Virginia campaign against Lee's army. He would not give up the field, nor would he break off his forces to give the enemy any extended relief. He had vowed to never stop, to fight against the Confederates in Virginia if it required him to attack throughout the entire summer of 1864. If the fighting on May 12 had not produced a major breakthrough, perhaps another day would do so.

Having failed to bring about a lasting break in the Confederate lines through a direct frontal assault, Grant set another strategy for May 13. As Lee had predicted before the battle had opened, the Federal Army began to move by its left again, heading southeast, continuing its arc around Richmond. To this end, Grant ordered Major General Gouverneur Warren's 5th Corps, placed on the army's right flank, to pull out of the Union line and march behind the army's front. They were to then position themselves on the left flank. General Horatio Wright's 6th Corps would then be in position as the new right flank of Grant's army. Then, Grant had Wright's forces do the same thing. This allowed the Army of the Potomac to move toward the southeast while always maintaining direct contact with Lee, presenting a constant, strong front.

There was little fighting during the several days following the May 12 Spotsylvania battle, just some minor engagements as the two armies squeezed against one another as the Union Army moved its positions southward. Grant did plan an attack on May 14, which was cancelled by heavy rains. Then, the

Union commander set a new course of attack, this time against Lee's left by the Federal right. Once again, Hancock's 2nd Corps, Wright's 6th, and Burnside's 9th attacked Lee's right in the early hours of May 18. But the Confederates in their path were well entrenched, and repeated assaults failed until Grant ordered a stand down. That evening, Grant returned to his strategy of moving by his left, which left Lee with little to do other than to match the Federals' moves.

On May 19, Lee sent General Ewell forward to examine whether Grant was, indeed, moving to the southeast again. As Ewell examined the Union left flank, a fight took place at Harris's Farm, which dragged on for the remainder of the day. Little was accomplished, but Ewell did determine Grant's intentions of moving by his left. As Union forces drew away from the landscape around Spotsylvania, the battle was finally over. In all the fighting during those days of mid-May, the Army of the Potomac suffered 17,500 casualties and Lee's army had 10,000 casualties.

The battle may have been over, but the fight continued on for several more weeks. There would be an engagement on May 23 to 25 along the North Anna River, south of Spotsylvania. Both sides bloodied one another until Grant again moved by his left flank to the southeast, closer to Richmond. On June 3, Grant sent thousands of his men to their doom when he attacked Lee in a direct frontal assault at Cold Harbor. The main attack at 4:30 that afternoon lasted little more than 30 minutes; it ended with 3,500 Union casualties.

Grant knew he had made a mistake at Cold Harbor. After that attack, he simply moved by his left, putting him southeast of Richmond and on a straight line with Petersburg, a vital rail center south of the Confederate capital. Here, the Union Army attacked Rebel forces defending the city on June 15. Even though the Union outnumbered the enemy by five to one, it failed to break through, due in part to the poor leadership of Union general William F. "Baldy" Smith.

For six weeks, Grant had pushed Lee's army, from the Wilderness to Petersburg. He had lost tens of thousands of men, killed and wounded, but he had managed to fight Lee to a standstill. Outside Petersburg, Grant simply laid down a siege, which would keep the Army of Northern Virginia locked up south of Richmond with no way out. The war had always been about fighting the Confederates until the South could no longer produce enough manpower to continue the war effectively. Through Grant's nonstop drive against Lee's forces in Virginia from spring until summer of 1864, the day of Confederate exhaustion had finally arrived.

Glossary

ARTILLERY   Large mounted guns or cannons; the part of an army that uses and manages such guns.

BRIGADE   A body of troops that generally includes two or more regiments or battalions, commanded by a brigadier general or a colonel. Usually part of a division.

CANISTER SHOT   A can containing hundreds of marble-sized lead projectiles that was fired from a cannon.

CARTRIDGE   A paper-wrapped measure of gunpowder that a soldier loaded in the barrel of his musket or rifle.

CASUALTY   In military terms, any human loss on a battlefield, including those killed, wounded, missing, and captured.

COMMISSION   An official granting of rank to a military officer.

CONFEDERATES   Those who supported secession from the United States and who fought for the South during the Civil War.

DIVISION   A military unit made up of several brigades or regiments plus supporting troops, usually commanded by a major general.

EMANCIPATION PROCLAMATION   An executive order issued by President Abraham Lincoln calling for the freeing of slaves in parts of the South engaging in secession and Civil War against the United States government.

FEDERALS   Troops who fought for the North, or the Union side, during the Civil War.

FLANK   Either end of a line of massed soldiers, signified as an army's "left" or "right."

GRAPE SHOT   A package of nine golf-ball-sized lead balls that were fired in one shot from the barrel of a cannon.

INSUBORDINATION   Resistance or disobedience to an authority; refusal to obey; disobedient or unruly behavior showing a lack of respect.

MEMOIRS   Personal narrative, remembrance, or autobiography that relates the writer's life story.

MINIE BALL   A cone-shaped projectile fired in a musket or rifle that was invented by a French army captain, Claude Minie.

MUSKET   A handheld weapon featuring a long smooth-bore barrel that fires a lead projectile or bullet.

MUZZLE   The far end of a musket or rifle barrel.

PONTOON BOATS   Flat-bottomed boats used to create a floating bridge across water.

REBELS   Commonplace term for Southerners who supported the Confederacy during the Civil War.

REGIMENT   A unit of an army made up of several battalions or squadrons of soldiers organized into one large group, usually commanded by a colonel.

RIFLE   A handheld weapon featuring a long barrel that fires a lead projectile or bullet.

RIFLE PITS   A term used to describe shallow trenches manned by riflemen.

SALIENT   A part of a fortification or line of trenches that projects toward the enemy.

SIEGE   The act of surrounding a fortified place by an army trying to capture it.

SKIRMISH   A small-scale military engagement with less scope or action than a full-fledged battle.

SUBORDINATE   An enlisted man serving under an officer of higher rank.

Bibliography

Bearss, Edwin C. *Fields of Honor: Pivotal Battles of the Civil War.* Washington, D.C.: National Geographic Society, 2006.

Catton, Bruce. *Grant Moves South.* Boston: Little, Brown & Company, 1960.

Catton, Bruce. *Grant Takes Command.* Boston: Little, Brown & Company, 1969.

Catton, Bruce. *Mr. Lincoln's Army.* Garden City, N.Y.: Doubleday and Company, 1951.

Cox, Samuel S. *Three Decades of Federal Legislation, 1855–1885.* Providence, R.I.: Harrington Press, 1885.

Cullen, Joseph. *Where a Hundred Thousand Fell: The Battles of Fredericksburg, Chancellorsville, the Wilderness, and Spotsylvania Court House.* Washington, D.C.: National Park Service, 1966.

Dennett, Tyler. *Lincoln and the Civil War in the Diaries and Letters of John Hay.* New York: Dodd, Mead & Company, 1939.

Dowdey, Clifford. *The Seven Days: The Emergence of Robert E. Lee.* Boston: Little, 1964.

Duke, John K. *History of the 53rd Ohio Volunteer Infantry.* Portsmouth, Ohio: Blade Print Co., 1900.

Foote, Shelby. *Civil War.* Vol. 2. New York: Random House, 1964.

Freeman, Douglas Southall. *R. E. Lee, a Biography.* Vols. 2 and 4. New York: Charles Scribner's Sons, 1934.

Henry, Robert S. *"First with the Most" Forrest.* Indianapolis: Bobbs-Merrill and Company, 1944.

Hill, D.H. "McClellan's Change of Base and Malvern Hill." In *Battles and Leaders of the Civil War,* Vol. 2, edited by Robert U. Johnson and Clarence C. Buell. New York: The Century Company, 1888.

Kennedy, Frances H., ed. *The Civil War Battlefield Guide.* Boston: Houghton Mifflin Company, 1990.

Longstreet, James. "The Battle of Fredericksburg." In *Battles and Leaders of the Civil War,* Vol. 3, edited by Robert U. Johnson and Clarence C. Buell. New York: The Century Company, 1888.

McDonough, James Lee. *Shiloh: In Hell Before Night*. Knoxville, Tenn.: University of Tennessee Press, 1977.

McPherson, James. *Battle Cry of Freedom: The Civil War Era*. New York: Oxford University Press, 1988.

Sears, Stephen, ed. *The Civil War: The Best of American Heritage*. Boston: Houghton Mifflin Company, 1991.

Thomas, Emory M. *Robert E. Lee, A Biography*. New York: W.W. Norton & Company, 1995.

Woodworth, Steve, and Kenneth J. Winkle. *Atlas of the Civil War*. New York: Oxford University Press, 2004.

Further Resources

Faust, Drew Gilpin. *This Republic of Suffering: Death and the American Civil War*. San Diego: Gale Group, 2008.

Ford, Carin T. *American Civil War: An Overview*. Berkeley Heights, N.J.: Enslow Publishers, 2004.

Kennedy, Robert, Jr. *American Heroes: Joshua Chamberlain and the American Civil War*. New York: Hyperion Books for Children, 2007.

McPherson, James. *Fields of Fury: The American Civil War*. New York: Simon & Schuster Children's Publishing, 2002.

Woodworth, Steven. *Cultures in Conflict: The American Civil War*. Westport, Conn.: Greenwood Publishing Group, 2000.

WEB SITES

American Civil War Museum
http://gettysburgmuseum.com/museum.asp

American Civil War Research Site
http://www.americancivilwar.com/civil.html

The American Civil War: The Battle of Gettysburg
http://www.brotherswar.com

CivilWar.com
http://www.civilwar.com

The Civil War Home Page
http://www.civil-war.net

Dakota State University: The American Civil War
http://homepages.dsu.edu/jankej/civilwar/battles.htm

Time Line of the Civil War
http://memory.loc.gov/ammem/cwphtml/tl1861.html

Picture Credits

Index

About
the Author

TIM MCNEESE is associate professor of history at York College in York, Nebraska, where he is in his seventeenth year of college instruction. Professor McNeese earned an associate of arts degree from York College, a bachelor of arts in history and political science from Harding University, and a master of arts in history from Missouri State University. A prolific author of books for elementary, middle school, high school, and college readers, McNeese has published more than 100 books and educational materials over the past 20 years, on everything from the founding of early New York to Hispanic authors. His writing has earned him a citation in the library reference work *Contemporary Authors* and multiple citations in *Best Books for Young Teen Readers*. In 2006, McNeese appeared on the History Channel program *Risk Takers, History Makers: John Wesley Powell and the Grand Canyon*. He was a faculty member at the 2006 Tony Hillerman Writers Conference in Albuquerque. His wife, Beverly, is an assistant professor of English at York College. They have two married children, Noah and Summer, and three grandchildren, Ethan, Adrianna, and Finn William. Tim and Bev McNeese sponsored study trips for college students on the Lewis and Clark Trail in 2003 and 2005, and to the American Southwest in 2008. You may contact Professor McNeese at tdmcneese@york.edu.